DREAMING THE DIVINE

THE INTIMATE CONNECTION
BETWEEN SLEEP AND SPIRITUALITY

Dream reality is a state between our world and the stars, between earth and sky, between the human experience and the goddesses and gods. Within its unlimited space, divine advice and prophetic messages can be acquired through direct communication with the deities, unhampered by the restraints of our waking reality.

Once, the connection between the physical and spiritual world was recognized and honored. Our society has let doubt and fear create an artificial barrier between the two realms, and too often we place our spiritual practices in the hands of others.

Seeking communion with the divine through dreams is one of the oldest forms of personal spirituality. Sacred sleep is one way to remove spirituality from the hands of the experts, and place it where it belongs: in the hearts, minds, and dreams of the worshippers themselves.

About the Author

Scott Cunningham learned about Wicca while still in high school, and practiced elemental magic for twenty years. He was the author of more than forty books, both fiction and non-fiction, sixteen of them published by Llewellyn Publications. He experienced, researched, then wrote about what he learned in his magical training. His books reflect a broad range of interests within the New Age sphere, where he was highly regarded. He passed from this life on March 28, 1993, after a long illness.

To Write to the Publisher

If you would like more information about this book, or other books by this author, please write to the publisher in care of Llewellyn Worldwide. The publisher appreciates hearing from you and learning of your enjoyment of this book and how it has helped you. Please write to:

Llewellyn Worldwide Ltd.
P.O. Box 64383, Dept. K192–9
St. Paul, MN 55164-0383, U.S.A.

Please enclose a self-addressed, stamped envelope for reply, or $1.00 to cover costs. If outside U.S.A., enclose international postal reply coupon.

DREAMING
THE
DIVINE

TECHNIQUES FOR SACRED SLEEP

Scott Cunningham

1999
Llewellyn Publications
St. Paul, Minnesota, 55164-0383, U.S.A.

SECOND EDITION
First Printing, 1999

(Formerly titled *Sacred Sleep: Dreams & the Divine*, published by Crossing Press, 1992)

Cover design by William Merlin Cannon
Interior art by Carrie Westfall
Editing and interior design by Connie Hill

Library of Congress Cataloging-in-Publication Data
Cunningham, Scott, 1956–1993
    Dreaming the divine : techniques for sacred sleep /
Scott Cunningham. — 2nd ed.
      p.   cm.
    Rev. ed. of: Sacred sleep. 1992.
    Includes bibliographical references and index.
    ISBN 1–56718–192–9
    1. Dreams.   2. Symbolism (Psychology).   3. Mental healing.
I. Cunningham, Scott, 1956–1993. II. Title.
BF1078.C86   1999
  99–0000
135'.3—dc21   99–39673
                                     CIP

Llewellyn Publications
A Division of Llewellyn Worldwide, Ltd.
P.O. Box 64383, Dept. K192–0
St. Paul, Minnesota 55164-0383, U.S.A.
www.llewellyn.com

 Printed in the United States of America

This book is dedicated to Those
who speak to us in the Night

Other Books by Scott Cunningham

A Formula Book of Magical Incenses and Oils
   A "Pixie Publishing" Production, 1982
   (Self-Published)
Magical Herbalism, 1982
Earth Power, 1983
Cunningham's Encyclopedia of Magical Herbs, 1985
The Magic of Incense, Oils, and Brews, 1986
   (Original Edition)
The Magical Household (with David Harrington),
   1987
Herb Magic (Videotape), 1987
The Truth About Witchcraft, 1987
The Truth About Witchcraft Today, *1988*
Wicca: A Guide for the Solitary Practitioner, 1988
The Complete Book of Incense, Oils, and Brews, 1989
   (Revised and expanded version of *The Magic of
   Incense, Oils, and Brews*)
The Magic in Food, 1991
The Truth About Herb Magic, 1992
Sacred Sleep (Crossing Press), 1992
The Art of Divination (Crossing Press), 1993
Living Wicca, 1993
Spell Crafts, 1993
Hawai'ian Religion and Magic, 1994
The Magic of Food, 1996
   (Revised edition of *The Magic in Food*)
Llewellyn's 1993 Magical Almanac,
   Editor, Contributor

CONTENTS

Contents

Contents

PREFACE

We spend almost one-third of our lives wrapped in shadows and dreams. Sleep provides rest for our bodies and our conscious minds. However, our inner beings are far from inactive during sleep, as is evidenced by our dreams.

Dreams have been the subject of spiritual and philosophical debate for 3,000 years. Such debate continues, particularly among sleep researchers who have as yet been unable to identify the mental and physiological processes at work during the occurrence of dreams. Though hundreds of theories have been advanced, dreams remain a mysterious, largely unexplained aspect of our daily lives.

Early polytheistic peoples had little difficulty in explaining dreams. There were some differences in these explanations, but most were founded on a belief unacceptable to the modern practice of scientific inquiry: dreams are spiritual experiences in which advice or warnings are issued from the divinities.

The intense interest in dreams has never waned. Thousands of books have been published, each promising to reveal the secrets of these night messages. Virtually all modern works, however, ignore the obvious spiritual nature of some dreams. The authors of these books prefer to see dreams as signs of unfulfilled wishes and past experiences. They boldly state that all dreams originate within their dreamers' minds and bodies. A few modern dream researchers grudgingly admit that some dreams seem to be of psychic origin, but all mention of dreams as messages from deity occur only in historical contexts, or are entirely dismissed.

This is a unique dream book. Though it acknowledges that some dreams lack deep meaning, it also embraces the concept that our personal deities can visit us in our dreams. Thus, sleep itself can be a spiritual act.

Part I of this book examines theories regarding dreams and their importance to the ancient Egyptians, Sumerians and Babylonians, Greeks, Romans, Hawaiians, and Native Americans. It closes with a short look at dream books.

Part II defines a unique ritual system designed to secure dreams from our personal deities, based on the techniques of antiquity as well as on personal experience. Part III consists of an in-depth guide to remembering and recording your dreams, interpreting them, and determining whether they're of divine origin.

Dreaming the Divine, then, is both an historical survey and a practical guide to this ancient process. It recognizes and celebrates the fact that, during sleep, we enter an alternate state of consciousness in which we're more easily approached by our goddesses and gods.

The techniques outlined in Parts II and III of this book aren't complex or time-consuming: a few actions, an invocation, bed. Yet they may well lead us to higher states of awareness, provide comfort and counselling, send warnings of the future, and strengthen our relationship with our personal deities.

Sleep can indeed be a ritual act. *Dreaming the Divine* is no less than a guide to a unique form of personal spiritual practice. Based on three millennia of the continuous use of similar rites, it elevates sleep from a necessary period of mental and physical rest to a higher purpose.

Dreaming the Divine has something to offer to all who worship the Goddess and the God.

Reveal yourself to me and let me see
a favorable dream.
May the dream that I dream be
favorable,
May the dream that I dream be true,
May Mamu, the goddess of dreams,
stand at my head;
Let me enter E-Sagila, the temple of
the gods, the house of life.

—Ancient Assyrian Dream Prayer

ACKNOWLEDGMENTS

To the goddesses who came to me in the night and assisted in the completion of this book;

To deTraci Regula, who answered technical questions concerning ancient Egypt and Rome, provided information concerning dream temples, loaned several scarce books, assisted with my research, commented on certain chapters, and tirelessly answered innumerable questions;

To Marilee Bigelow, who provided information concerning Egyptian deities, commented on certain chapters, and who was largely responsible for my early introduction to many ancient religions and cultures;

And to my computer, for not breaking down. All errors in presenting or interpreting historic material remain, of course, my own.

Chapter 1

The Mysteries of Dreams

The visions that come to us in the night can be so puzzling, informative, frightening, or interesting that virtually every major culture has lent them great significance. Some peoples determined that dreams were caused by demons; others, by divinities. Dreams were explained as memories of the temporarily detached human soul's wanderings during sleep; as messages from deceased relatives; as pure creative fantasies; even as the mind sorting through recent events during sleep. At least one early culture found that dreams were subconscious "soul" urges brought to the conscious mind during sleep.

What can we make of this welter of conflicting concepts? Perhaps we should begin by examining the nature of human consciousness.

THE TWO MINDS

Mystics throughout the ages have postulated that we possess two minds: the conscious mind, which we use during our daily activities, and the subconscious (or psychic) mind, which is in control during sleep. (Recent theories regarding the separate functions of the brain's two hemispheres seem to be in harmony with this theory.)

The conscious mind is proficient at adding figures, reading, theorizing, instructing the body to perform exacting tasks, driving, and for other activities. It awakens with us and slips into repose during the night. It is concerned with the material world, with verbal and written communications, financial matters, and other mundane concerns.

Our society places great importance on the conscious mind. By it, we've created our civilizations, customs, languages, technological advances, legal systems, and every other aspect of our daily waking lives. Education is largely a matter of training our conscious minds to act in harmony with other conscious minds. The subconscious mind is far more mysterious. It resides within the realm of sleep, dreams, spirituality, psychic awareness and intuition. The psychic mind usually rises from its daily sleep only when we lie still in the night (though hunches may be messages from this realm of consciousness).

When we're awake, the conscious mind blocks communication with the subconscious mind. It simply doesn't allow information from the other mind to intrude into our waking life. This is a direct result of many of the teachings that we receive early in life: "Don't daydream." "Pay attention." "Concentrate!" "There's no such thing as psychic awareness."

Some individuals are able to utilize their psychic minds during waking hours: psychics, sensitives, mystics, artists, and writers. There can be no doubt that the psychic mind is also at work during spiritual and religious rituals. Still, we're usually not even aware of its presence—except within our dreams.

Dreams are often perceived to be irrational or fantastic, precisely because they aren't under the control of the conscious mind. The dream-state is not limited by time or space; it operates within an alternate reality. In our dreams, the dead may appear; we may visit distant places and move through water like a fish or fly like a bird. Freed from all physical laws, the subconscious mind takes us on deeply symbolic journeys.

SYMBOLISM

Symbolism is the language of the subconscious mind. Thus, though we may walk, speak, and perform many other actions in dreams, symbols usually appear as veiled messages. The origin of such symbols may be the subconscious mind itself; psychic impulses received during sleep; even the deity or deities whom we worship.

These dream symbols (rain, circles, numbers, animals, plants, colors, etc.) usually bear important messages or information that would be blocked during wakefulness. All psychologists and mystics are aware of this phenomenon, although they have differing opinions as to the nature of these messages. The interpretation of dreams is largely a matter of examining the symbols that appear within them (see Chapter 14).

Our personal dream languages differ from those we use in everyday communication and thought. Fortunately, they possess their own structures and logic. Each person's inner being, emotions, spirituality, and personal experience determines the nature of her or his dream symbols. Not all dream symbols are meaningful, but all meaningful dream symbols are direct attempts to speak to our conscious minds.

Types of Dreams

Dreams have been classified in a number of categories. The following sections briefly describe these major categories. Further information may be found in Chapter 14.

Natural Dreams

Natural dreams are also known as wish-fulfillment, fantasy, and entertainment dreams. They bear no deep messages; no hidden meanings; no prophecies of the future. Natural dreams are created by our wishes and hopes. Information derived from movies, television, books, and magazines may also be integrated into natural dreams. Such dreams may be interesting, but they're of little weight.

Psychic Dreams

One of the most famous American psychic dreams occurred to Abraham Lincoln. One night, asleep in bed, he dreamed of his impending death. Not long after this disturbing incident, he went to the Ford Theater where he was fatally wounded.[1]

Psychic dreams are those which present information regarding future events from as-yet unexplained sources. These messages aren't received through any of the five "normal" senses, but through the subconscious (psychic) mind.

Such dreams are quite common among persons of all educational backgrounds, races, and religions. They occur to persons of all ages.

The theory is quite simple: psychic information is received by the subconscious mind during sleep. The mind then translates the information into meaningful symbols, perhaps by constructing a mental image similar to that revealed in the message: a plane crashes; an earthquake jars the house;

a friend visits; or a long-awaited letter arrives. Alternately, the message may be received in the form of words spoken by a familiar or unknown person. Psychic dreams are rather rare, but most of us have experienced at least one.

Telepathic Dreams

The possibility of what we would term "telepathic" dreams was expressed by the Greek scientist Democritus, who wrote that dreams could be the result of "emanations" from other persons and objects entering the consciousness during sleep.[2] This view is still highly regarded by non-scientists, although it is usually limited to the penetration of other person's thoughts during sleep. Telepathy (the direct transference of thought between humans) remains a controversial area of study.

Telepathic dreams could, in part, explain psychic dreams. Thought messages received from dying relatives or endangered friends could trigger dreams. Much study remains to be done.

As an aside, some studies have shown that sixty to seventy percent of those who claim to have experienced telepathy stated that they did so in dreams.[3]

Astral Projection Dreams

Most ancient cultures saw sleep as a period when the human soul was temporarily released from the body. In sleep, the soul wandered, exploring this and other worlds, meeting with deities and with other human souls. This ancient concept is today known as astral projection. Some feel that certain dreams may be the remembrances of unconsciously controlled astral projection. Such dreams are often highly fictitious, for we see what we wish to see in the astral realm.

Divine Dreams

Divine dreams are those that are given by the sleeper's personal deity (or deities). Dreams have always been linked with spirituality. Sleep is the perfect time for our divinities to make Their presences known and to offer comfort or guidance. The doubting mind is stilled. The body is motionless. The subconscious mind is in full operation, and thus can easily receive messages from the divine.

Divinely inspired dreams aren't merely relics of Pagan religions. Early Christians accepted that "God" could inspire dreams. Origen, St. Augustine, St. Thomas Aquinas, and many other early

Christian figures wrote that interpreting the future through dreams wasn't spiritually unlawful, for God instructed humans through dreams. The Bible is filled with accounts of divine dreams.[4]

Divine dreams could occur on any night, without warning. Some cultures also supported the use of magical/religious rites designed to create divine dreams in times of need. And finally, such dreams could be inspired by sleeping in temples.

DREAM INCUBATION (SACRED SLEEP)

Dreams were so highly valued as divine messages that dream temples enjoyed enormous popularity in the ancient world. Egypt, Babylon, Greece, and Rome supported thousands of temples devoted to this art.

Dream incubation (from the Latin: *incubare*) is a technical term describing the creation of sacred dreams for a specific purpose: healing, advice, glimpses of the future, protection, conception of children, battle plans, and a host of other reasons. Every free citizen of these nations could visit a temple, make an offering (or an animal sacrifice), and spend the night on divine ground. The fortunate awoke in the morning in the possession of a dream from the deity that answered her or his prayers.

The theories underlying the once widespread practice of dream incubation are clear.

+ The divinities are concerned about Their worshippers

+ Dreams can be sent by goddesses and gods

+ The nearest that a worshipper can be to a deity, while in a corporeal state, is within the confines of Her or His temple

+ Thus, sleeping within the temple will be the most effective method of producing a divine dream

The origins of dream incubation (also known as temple sleep and sacred sleep) are unknown. It might have been independently developed in Sumer and Egypt. There can be little doubt that the practice of temple sleep later spread to Babylon and Assyria, then greatly influenced similar practices in Greece and the Roman empire. Similar forms of dream incubation were in common use among many Native American tribes (see Chapter 7), pre-Christian Hawaiians (Chapter 6), Australian aborigines, and throughout Africa. Dream incubation continues as a structured religious practice in contemporary Japan. Sacred sleep was once a world-wide practice.[5]

MODERN DREAM THEORIES

In 1899, Sigmund Freud published *The Interpretation of Dreams*, in which he stated that all present pathological mental conditions could be explained by inner sexual conflict and frustration. (He later altered this to include all manners of conflicts and frustrated wishes.) Freud soon realized that one method of unlocking these buried memories was through the analysis of his patients' dreams.

For years, his book was largely ignored and his theories were dismissed.[6] Still, Freud continued and ideveloped psychoanalysis, as we know it today (which still isn't accepted by many experts).

Scientific research into the nature of dreams was rare until the late 1950s and the early 1960s. Then a group of scientists studying sleep discovered a possible correlation between rapid eye movement (REM) and dreams during sleep. This discovery was widely hailed as the first physiological evidence linking the body with dreams.

However, later studies showed that the correlation between REM and dreams was insignificant. By awakening patients in both REM and non-REM states, researchers discovered that dreams could occur at many points in sleep: REM wasn't necessary for the production of dreams.[7]

Studies continued. Theories were advanced regarding the nature of dreams (usually divorced from physiological factors). Among the currently accepted theories are: dreams represent the assimilation of anxieties; they are nighttime struggles to overcome problems; dreams depict the integration of new information (from books, newspapers, television, movies); or are methods by which the mind releases useless information.[8]

Chapter 2

EGYPT

Humans have lived continuously on the lush land that surrounds the Nile for at least 6,000 years. The first known settlements in the Nile valley date from the Paleolithic era, but no direct connection has been found between these extremely early inhabitants and the latterday Egyptians.

The Dynastic period began in about 2950 B.C.E.[1] (In this book I've used the abbreviations B.C.E. and C.E. for "Before the Common Era" and "Common Era," the nonreligious equivalents of

B.C. and A.D., respectively.) Permanent cities were established, engendering the need for the production of food, trade, a common written language, a calendar (for both religious and civil purposes), mathematics and geometry (for trade and architecture), government social structures, a legal code, the collection of taxes (to support the government), and, of course, structured religious rituals as well as magic.

Evolving from these practical activities were literature, lyric poetry (both sacred and secular), sculpture, masonry, painting, advanced pottery, brewing, metalwork, and a host of other arts.

The elite Egyptian upper class enjoyed a fairly luxurious life, considering that Egypt was situated in the middle of a merciless desert. They often lived in uncluttered houses with walled gardens that sported fish ponds, potted plants, and neatly clipped trees. Most upper-class homes contained a private temple or niche at which the family's deities were worshipped on a daily basis.

The lower classes certainly didn't live in such luxury, but during its nearly 3,000-year history Egypt experienced many periods of war and civil discontent, resulting in widespread privation and suffering for persons of all social classes. Every Egyptian shared the burden of living in one of the most coveted land areas in the Middle East.

However, in times of plenty, music, dance, feasts and parties enlivened the Egyptians' everyday existence. Cosmetics (eyeliner, lipstick, skin softeners, and fingernail paints) were in constant use by those who could afford them.[2] Perfumes (solid and liquid) were extensively used by both men and women.[3] Baths were perfumed with flowers and scented vegetable oils.[4] The Egyptians stand as one of the most cultured civilizations ever to emerge on earth.

Egyptian state religion was polytheistic. A large pantheon of goddesses and gods were worshipped. Many of these were recognized only in specific cities; some fell in and out of favor through the centuries, and others were widely worshipped. State and civil religious rituals involved the use of sacred tools, offerings of food and beverages (including bread, milk, beer, and animals), spices and incense, and lengthy invocation. Processions, music, and dancing accompanied many public rituals. Priestesses and priests attached to temples led decorous rites, often involving thousands of persons. Fragrant incense smoke perfumed the air.

Unfortunately, little information concerning personal religion in ancient Egypt remains, simply because most of its practitioners lacked the ability to write, and the temple scribes were far too busy to concern themselves with such matters. Their works offer little insight into personal religious practice. However, we can find clues by examining the importance of dreams in ancient Egypt.

EGYPTIAN DREAMING

Dreams were an important aspect of Egyptian religion.[5] The Roman author Diodorus stated that, in Egypt, "dreams are regarded with religious reverence";[6] the unknown author of *Instructions for Merikare* (circa 2100 B.C.E.); wrote that dreams are sent by the deities so that their worshippers may know the future;[7] demotic inscriptions in Nubia attest to the divine inspiration of dreams,[8] and there are other ancient proofs.

Few written works concerning dreams survive from the earliest Dynastic periods. However, comparing these fragmented records with the Roman writings of the Ptolemaic period, it becomes clear that dreams were considered an important source of information originating from the dreamer's personal deity.[9] Healing techniques, warnings of future dangers, reassurances of divine love, friendly advice, and answers to the dreamer's questions were all received in the form of dreams.[10]

Thus, it seems safe to state that Egyptians viewed sleep as a sacred ritual in which worshippers were intimately united with their personal deities.

The Nature of Egyptian Dreaming

No evidence remains to suggest that the Egyptians recognized the separation of the soul from the body during sleep.[11] To them, dreams weren't memories of astral wandering, but were experiences (both spiritual and mundane) that took place in a separate realm that hid itself during wakefulness.[12]

The Egyptians apparently divided dreams into three categories. The first of these could be termed "pious" dreams, in which deities appear and demand or ask (depending on the deity's temperament) that their worshipper perform some act of piety.[13] Such dreams seem to have been largely limited to pharaohs, generals, and other high officials, and can be viewed as tests of the worshipper's devotion to her or his deity.

A few examples of such pious dreams have survived. While he was a young man, Thutmose IV went hunting in his chariot for lions and wild goats. Exhausted, he fell asleep in the shadow of the Sphinx. Through neglect, this impressive monument had been partially buried in the sand. While Thutmose slept, the god Hamarkis,[14] who may have been the deity originally depicted in the Sphinx,[15] appeared to him. Hamarkis promised the young prince that if he dug the Sphinx from the sands and re-established the temple created for Hamarkis' worship, Thutmose would be pharaoh.[16]

Thutmose IV did indeed perform these tasks, and in due time became ruler of Egypt. He recorded his dream on a famous stele that sits between the Sphinx's paws. Unfortunately, the final portion of the story is missing.[17] Indeed, even the extant stele may be only an ancient copy of the original.

In some dreams, deities appeared and demanded a pious task, but offered nothing in return. Their worshippers, out of love or respect for the goddesses and gods, usually performed the requested task. Plutarch records an instance of this. Ptolemy Soter once dreamed of an immense statue. In his dream, Serapis told Ptolemy Soter to find the statue and to bring it to Alexandria. Immediately upon waking, he organized several search parties, the statue was located and returned to the city.[18]

The next most important group of dreams were those that could be termed "revelatory"; ie. dreams that pointed to future events, warned of impending disaster, and revealed appropriate medicines or the hiding places of papyri and other valuable objects.[19] Such messages were viewed as stemming from the dreamer's personal deity.

Some dreams were simply informational. One authority refers to two late examples in which the goddess Hathor appeared to worshippers in dreams. In one dream, Hathor appeared to a man and directed him, within his dream, to the best location for his tomb.[20]

EGYPTIAN TEMPLE SLEEP AND DREAM INCUBATION

Egyptians slept overnight in temples to receive divinely inspired dreams. After purification and sacrifice, the worshipper retired for the evening. During this sacred sleep she or he received a message from the temple's attendant deity.

Such dreams could be directly responsible for providing glimpses into the future, warnings of danger, even success in love and business. A dream may have also, at times, been designed to spiritually uplift the deity's dreamer, a divine reassurance that the worshipper was walking the right path.

What may have begun as an isolated religious rite, limited to a few temples, spread throughout Egypt and became enormously popular. Many temples were famous for the messages received during sacred sleep. Among these were the temples of Isis on the island of Philae[21] and at Koptos;[22] of Imhotep at Memphis,[23] of Seti I at Abydos;[24] of Thoth at Hermopolis;[25] of Serapis at Alexandria;[26] of Ptah Sotmu at Memphis;[27] and the temple of Amon-Ra in the Lybian desert, twelve days journey from Memphis.[28] The popularity of Serapis as a provider of dreams (He was first recognized in the Ptolemaic period)[29] may indicate that dream incubation swelled to its enormous popularity somewhat late in Egyptian history.

Egyptian dream incubation's original function may have been to receive a method of healing (a medicine, a prayer), or to receive an actual healing during sleep directly from the deity. This was certainly true of the temples of Isis, Whose powers were so great that She was described as the "healer of all diseases."[30]

An Example of an Incubated Dream

Mehitousket, the wife of a famous Egyptian magician, Setme Khamuas, had never been pregnant, so she slept in the temple of Imhotep.[31] In her dream, she was instructed to make a medicine from a plant and administer this to her husband.[32] She followed this advice and the remedy succeeded: she gave birth to a son. Setme Khamuas received the son's name in a dream, and the boy grew to be a great magician.[33]

Procedures in the Dream Temples

Temples in which incubation took place weren't solely used for such purposes, of course. The priestesses, priests, and the temple's general staff also presided over a large number of daily rituals, counseled the sick and depressed, and performed other duties. Some temples resembled small towns, with barbers, gardeners, brewers, and other tradespeople in attendance.

From the extant fragmentary knowledge we can create a picture of the procedures that took place in the dream oracle temples. Most temples were open to both rich and poor, the young and old, the sick and the healthy, and women and men.[34] The worshipper arrived at the temple, sometimes on her or his own volition, occasionally as the result of a previous dream in which the deity stated that she or he should visit. Absolute faith in the deity's power and influence were prerequisites.[35]

Judging from later Ptolemaic Egyptian practices, a purification of some kind probably followed. Absolute purity (probably a reference to no recent sexual congress) was a requirement for dream incubation.[36] The worshipper might be instructed to fast or to take mixtures that induced beneficial dreams.[37]

The rituals began. These were led by the temple's clergy (many of whom were women, and some of whom served exclusively as dream clergy).[38] The supplicant almost assuredly offered some sort of sacrifice (bloodless or otherwise). Invocation of the deity by the clergy then followed. Some of these prayers may have also been uttered by the patient for the deity was appealed to "hear the prayer" and to reveal Her or His presence to the worshipper ("Turn Your face towards me").[39]

Prayers also commonly included such pious statements as:

> *You Who accomplishes miracles and are benevolent in all your doings.* (Particularly apt for healing.)

> *You Who gives children to her [or him] who has none.* (Sterility; barrenness.)

> *You Who can grant the means of saving all.*

The deity was then entreated to appear in the sleeper's dream and reveal the necessary information. Such prayers were probably made directly to the statue of the deity itself, as it was the closest earthly representation of the goddess or god.

The worshipper then slept within the temple itself. If the deity so chose, She or He appeared and often addressed the worshipper by name.[40] Once this identification had been made, the goddess or god proceeded to answer the supplicant's question. The dream-answer was sometimes quite explicit.[41] At other times, the message was couched in deep symbolism.[42] In either case, the worshipper usually awoke spiritually refreshed, ready to unravel the nature of the message.

Dream Interpretation

Dreams couched in mystic symbolism had, of necessity, to be interpreted. Assisting the dreamers were either a special class of dream-interpretation clergy,[43] or simply the temple's spiritual staff, who would be intimately familiar with the symbols and the forms in which the deities usually appeared.

The temple clergy unlocked the veiled messages of the temple's deity. Interpretation of some symbols (snakes, birds, amulets and other objects directly connected with the deity's worship) were probably quite simple. However, at least one dream book from ancient Egypt has survived, and this suggests that such books may have been used for either temple or private use.

Dream books are catalogues of symbols or actions that appear in dreams, with their attendant interpretations (see Chapter 8). The Egyptian example (known as the *Chester Beatty Papyrus III*) was found in Thebes, written in approximately 1350 B.C.E.[44] Internal evidence shows that this book is a compilation of earlier material, some of which probably dates back to as early as 2000 B.C.E.[45]

The *Chester Beatty Papyrus III* offers us a fascinating glimpse into Egyptian dream symbolism. Some

108 dreams and their interpretations are recorded in this papyrus, which also includes a spell to avert the effects of "bad" dreams.[46] Unfortunately, the papyrus has been damaged, so the book's introductory material and closing statements have been lost. What remains are the interpretations themselves.[47]

The Beatty papyrus is neatly written in hieratic script. Running down the right margin (the papyrus was read from right to left) are various dream symbols or actions. The left side of the papyrus contains the interpretations. Each interpretation begins with either the word "good" or "bad";[48] the good interpretations were written in black ink and the bad interpretations were written in red ink, as the word itself was considered inauspicious.[49]

Curiously, a separate section in this work interprets dreams given to worshippers of Set. Only the introduction to this section has remained; the interpretations themselves have not survived.[50] This is the only distinction made for worshippers of a specific deity in the entire work. Based purely on inductive reasoning, it seems likely that the Beatty papyrus' compiler was a Set worshipper, or was at least familiar with this group, and so recorded such dreams. Each deity may have possessed unique dream interpretations for Her or His worshippers, all of which have been lost.

The interpretations recorded in the Beatty papyrus are somewhat one dimensional. One authority[51] suggests that the dream book was either a training manual for new dream interpreters, or was designed for private use by those few persons who could read; another states that the Chester Beatty papyrus is closer to literature than to a manual for practical use.[52] We can't know the papyrus' true reason for existence until or unless additional examples are found, and the papyri are compared.

Following are some of the dreams from the Beatty papyrus, together with their meanings. (The constant references to the dreamer as "he" may have been inserted by Sir Alan Gardiner, the work's translator; we have no evidence that these dreams had meaning solely for men.):

Killing an ox: Good. Removal of the dreamer's enemies from his presence.[53]

Writing on a palette: Good. Establishment of the dreamer's office.[54]

Picking dates: Good. Food will be given by this deity.[55]

Seeing a large cat: Good. A large harvest is coming to the dreamer.[56]

Uncovering the buttocks: Bad. The dreamer will become an orphan.[57] (This was a play on words: the Egyptian word for "buttocks" resembles the word for "orphan."[58] Such word play in Egyptian dream analysis was apparently quite common.[59])

Drinking wine: Good. The dreamer lives in righteousness.[60]

Seeing his face as a leopard: Good. Authority will be gained over his townspeople.[61]

Seeing himself as dead: Good. It means a long life.[62]

Carving an ox with his hands: Good. It means killing his adversary.[63]

Veiling himself: Good. Enemies will be removed from his presence.[64]

Copulating with a pig: Bad. He will be deprived of his possessions.[65]

Sawing wood: Good. His enemies will die.[66]

Teeth falling out: Bad. Death at the hands of his dependents.[67]

Catching birds: Bad. Some possessions will be lost.[68]

Seeing a snake: Good. A dispute will be settled.[69]

Filling pots: Bad. A great loss.[70]

Pouring beer from a vessel: Bad. The dreamer will be robbed.[71]

As can be seen in the above selection of Egyptian dream interpretations, the Egyptians accepted that seemingly positive dream symbols were often interpreted in negative ways; negative symbols, in positive ways. The death of the dreamer as a sign of long life is an excellent example. This concept was also accepted in ancient Greece and Rome, and has persisted to the present day.

Magically Produced Dreams

That magic and dreams were linked is made abundantly clear by an ancient papyrus in the Hermitage. It states that one of the reasons for Isis' creation of magic was to arm humans with an effective weapon against the dangers encountered during either sleep or wakefulness.[72]

A few ancient Egyptian rituals designed to produce divinely inspired dreams have survived.[73] One of these is quite famous. Certain names are written upon a piece of linen. The linen is folded to create a lamp wick, is soaked with oil, set into a lamp, and set aflame.[74] The practitioner refrains from food. An incantation is pronounced seven times before the lamp. The lamp is extinguished and the practitioner lies down to sleep.[75]

Though such dream rituals were usually performed at home, magicians could also be consulted for assistance. Prayers, spells, and the manipulation of unusual objects (special inks; the writing of secret symbols and the like) sum up these rituals. The deity was, as usual, entreated to send a dream to the worshipper.[76]

BES AND DREAMS

Bes seems to have been one of the most popular personal deities in ancient Egypt. Usually depicted as a naked dwarf with a flat face and bowed legs, Bes was the patron of music and art,[77] and protected women during childbirth.[78] He was also invoked before sleep to send pleasant dreams[79] and to guard the sleeper against nightmares.[80] Small ceramic images of Bes were hung over headrests,[81] or His image was carved onto the headrest itself to guard against the approach of evil spirits during sleep.[82]

Bes was also specifically invoked to send prophetic dreams.[83] To obtain a dream from Bes, the worshipper mixed a magical ink composed of such ingredients as frankincense, myrrh, rain water, cinnabar, mulberry juice, and wormwood juice, mixed with normal black ink.[84]

The worshipper used this ink to draw a picture or symbol of Bes on her or his left hand. The right hand was wrapped in one end of a long strip of black cloth that may have been consecrated to Isis. Silence was maintained as the worshipper reclined for sleep. At this point the remainder of the black cloth was wound around the neck and, sleeping in this somewhat unusual posture, the worshipper would then experience a vision of Bes in a dream.[85]

Magical Removal of the Effects of Harmful Dreams

If a warning of impending disaster appeared in a dream, the worshipper, naturally, prayed to her or his deity to be released from the foretold danger. Perhaps a second dream would be incubated or magically produced to receive the deity's advice on avoiding the predicted unhappy future.

Spells to ensure that dreams did not come true were also used in temple incubation. One extant example sums up the nature of these spells. Upon waking from a terrifying dream, the dreamer was instructed by the clergy to pray to Isis to drive away the evil forces (or to, in some other manner, prevent the dream's manifestation). The worshipper was presented with bread moistened with beer and myrrh, which the dreamer immediately smeared on her or his face.[86] Beer and bread were probably used in this Isian spell because both are sacred to Isis, the divine brewer.

It is clear that personal religion among the ancient Egyptians was profoundly affected by sleep and dreaming. The deities united with their worshippers during sleep. The deities were also invoked to guard the sleeper and to produce dreams. Healings occurred during temple sleep. Dreams were one of the few methods that humans possessed of entering the presence of their deities.

The goddesses and gods of ancient Egypt did not exist atop high, inaccessible mountains. They surrounded their worshippers with love, caring, and support, and communicated their concern through the agency of dreams.

Chapter 3

THE MIDDLE EAST: SUMER, BABYLON, AND ASSYRIA

The Sumerians were an extraordinary, non-Semitic people, remarkable for their original achievements in law, education, social reform, medicine, agriculture, philosophy, architecture, and literature.[1] Even more remarkable is that the very existence of this people remained unknown until about 140 years ago,[2] when archaeologists looking for Assyrian sites began stumbling on surprising evidence of an even older culture. The evidence slowly grew. In 1850, an esteemed archaeologist read a paper in which he expressed doubt that the Assyrians and Babylonians had invented cuneiform writing.[3]

Until this time, most Middle Eastern archaeology had been focused on proving the veracity of the Bible, and only Semitic cultures (Babylon, Assyria, Akkad) were studied. The possibility that a non-Semitic culture had predated Babylon seemed absurd, for none was mentioned in the Bible. The ensuing arguments led to archaeological digs in Iraq. The artifacts and buildings found there finally established the existence of Sumer.[4] Many other excavations followed.

Sumerian archaeology continued to be hampered by closed-minded archaeologists for several decades. Soon, however, the overwhelming linguistic and plastic remains of an ancient non-Semitic culture could no longer be denied, and Sumer made the history books.

SUMER

The first settlements in Sumer date from about 4500 B.C.E.[5] For 2,750 years, Sumer dominated Mesopotamia, producing a rich philosophical culture. Unfortunately, we know little concerning early Sumerian history. The Sumerians lacked the concept of historical evaluation and, indeed, thought that most events were determined and executed by their deities—without the assistance of humans.[6] The earliest records are solely related to religious offerings and to rulers' construction of temples. Still, it is possible to formulate some ideas concerning the Sumerians' conceptions of religion and dreams.

Sumerian Religion

Sumerian religion was polytheistic. The first deities sprang directly from nature: the sun, moon, sky, clouds, earth, sea, water, wind, rivers, mountains, plains, and other forces and realms.[7] Tools vital to life in ancient Sumer were also associated with deities.[8] The divinities created all that was in existence through the manifesting power of their divine words.[9]

The Sumerians thought that humans were created for a single purpose: to serve and to worship the deities.[10] Life was a series of doubts and fears concerning the future. Even death offered no release: the spirits of the deceased traveled to a dreary underworld filled with darkness, where existence was even more dismal than that enjoyed on earth.[11] There seems to have been no trace of the concept of reincarnation. Indeed, the Sumerians termed the underworld "the land of no return."[12]

The Sumerian deities were seen as completely anthropomorphic beings,[13] though they were far more powerful than any human. Deities enjoyed food and drink (hence, the food offerings). They married, raised children, supported households and exhibited all the virtues and weaknesses of humans.[14]

The Sumerians may have been the first civilization to recognize a personal deity, through which contact with higher deities could be accomplished.[15] The greatest goddesses and gods (An, the heaven god; Enlil, the wind god; Ninhursag, the great Mother Goddess; and Enki, the god of wisdom) were simply too powerful and had far too many duties to be directly concerned with human desires. Thus, they were approached through personal divinities, who perhaps had less responsibility and could, therefore, be contacted by individual worship rather than through state rituals.[16]

Though acts of personal piety (prayer, offerings, and so on) were highly regarded,[17] temple rituals were considered to be of greater importance. Each city-state boasted a tutelary deity and temple, and it was this deity that in large part protected those who lived within its confines. Temples dedicated to specific deities date back to at least 3000 B.C.E.[18]

Dreams Among the Sumerians

Little Sumerian dream information has survived. We do know that these people accepted the divine origination of at least some dreams. It is possible that the deity was thought to enter into the dreamer's consciousness through an opening in the head, for some texts state that the dream-providing deity "stood" at the dreamer's head.[19]

The first recorded divine Sumerian dream was experienced by Eannatum, the Sumerian ruler of the city-state Lagash. In about 2450 B.C.E., Eannatum recorded that his personal god, Ningirsu, "stood at his head" while he was sleeping and, in a dream, informed him that during his upcoming war with the city of Umma, the king of Kish would support neither side.[20]

Other clues can be gleaned from a religious poem that was preserved on two cylinders excavated at Lagash. These documents represent the longest known Sumerian written work in existence. Included in this narrative are accounts of the divine dreams of Gudea (who ruled Lagash from 2199–2180 B.C.E.). In a dream, Gudea sees a tall male figure, wearing a divine crown. Wings sprout from his shoulders and lions crouch to the figure's right and left.[21]

The sun quickly rises in the dream. A woman appears to Gudea, holding a stylus of gold and a clay tablet bearing a sketch of the stars. She is followed by a "hero" bearing a lapis lazuli tablet. The hero draws the plans for a temple on the tablet. Nearby, a male donkey is pawing the earth.[22]

When he awakes, Gudea is extremely puzzled by this dream, so he journeys to the temple of Nanshe, the goddess Who interprets divine dreams. Once at Her temple, Gudea makes his offerings and prays, then sleeps. In his sleep, he relates the troubling dream to Nanshe:

> *Something has come to me in the night*
> *watches; its meaning I know not. . . . May*
> *the prophetess, She Who has the knowledge*
> *of what pertains to me; may my Goddess*
> *Nanshe reveal to me its importance . . .*
> *O Nanshe, O Queen,*

> *O mistress of unfathomable decrees . . . your*
> *word is faithful and shines most brightly.*
> *You are the prophetess of the divinities . . .*
> *O Mother Interpretress of Dreams,*
> *in the midst of my dreams I saw . . .* [23]

Gudea relates his dream. Then, Nanshe interprets it for him: the large man was the god Ningirsu, Nanshe says; He commanded Gudea to build a
new temple for His worship. Dawn represented
Gudea's personal deity: Ningishzida. The woman
with the stylus and clay tablet was Nisaba (goddess of writing); the stars appearing on Her tablet
were a divine command to build the temple
according to the "holy stars" (possibly a reference
to astrological considerations).

The "hero" bearing the lapis lazuli tablet was
Nindub (an architect god), who naturally drew the
plan for the new temple. Finally, the male donkey
scratching at the earth was Gudea himself, represented as being impatient to do these deities'
commands. After waking, Gudea offered a sacrifice,
found its omens positive, and carried out Ningirsu's
instructions.[24]

This account is invaluable, for it reveals several
aspects of Sumerian dreaming (see p. 42).

✦ Dreams could be received from deities

✦ Several deities could appear in a dream, all connected with the dream's message

✦ The dreamer's personal deity was also likely to be present

✦ Dream symbolism could be puzzling; in this case, deities could be asked to interpret the dream; in addition, one class of Sumerian priests, the *ensi*, specialized in the interpretation of dreams[25]

✦ Some form of dream incubation existed in Sumer; because all human actions and their futures were determined by the deities, it seems reasonable that worshippers visited temples to learn at least part of these divine plans; however, dream incubation was not necessarily an all-purpose method of receiving divine guidance; as the story of Gudea indicates, people may have gone to the temple for this purpose most often after receiving a puzzling dream elsewhere

✦ The dreamer herself or himself may be represented in symbolic form in the dream

✦ Sacrifices were made after dream incubation

Further insight into Sumerian dreams can be garnered from a text entitled "The Death of Dumuzi" (circa 1750 B.C.E.). In this work, Dumuzi, the shepherd god of Erech, has a premonition of his own death. He ventures out onto the wild plain, falls sleep, and dreams of a terrifying and ominous experience. Upon waking, finding himself unable to unlock the dream's symbolism, Dumuzi calls his sister, Geshtinanna (the famous goddess of divine dream interpretation, as well as a poetess and singer), to interpret his dream.[26] Alas, She states that it is an omen of His death. How the deities could die has been left unexplained by early Sumerian scribes, though this may be a clue to their human origins.

This text adds further information to our survey of dreams in Sumer: even the goddesses and gods dreamed and could experience difficulty in interpreting Their night visions.

Goddesses as Dream Interpreters

From information culled from these sources and from the epic Sumerian poem, *Gilgamesh*, we're left with the strong impression that the Sumerian deities associated with dream interpretation were all goddesses: Nanshe, Geshtinanna, and Ninsun (mentioned in *Gilgamesh*). Admittedly, texts from ancient Sumer are scarce, but it seems safe to state that, though gods could appear in dreams, male deities didn't offer dream interpretation in Sumer.

BABYLON AND ASSYRIA

Babylon arose as an independent political power following a change in the climate of the region. Its establishment was apparently made possible by the receding of the Tigris River, which exposed a large section of fertile land, previously uninhabitable, lying both north and east of the well-established cities of the Sumerian empire. Settlements of Semitic peoples began in approximately 2371 B.C.E.,[27] and several cultures developed.

The first major civilization to take root in what was later known as Babylon was Akkad (named for the capital city). In direct contrast to Sumer, the Akkadians were a Semitic people. They quickly conquered Sumer—although certain aspects of Sumerian culture persisted, the city-states of Sumer were no longer independent.

The period of Akkadian rule was rather short—about 141 years.[28] However, it is of great importance for it was the Akkadians who first introduced early Semitic (non-Hebrew) elements into Sumerian religious practices.

A people known as the Gutians overthrew the Akkadians, but they were, in turn, driven out by the Sumerians, who reestablished their culture. This new Sumerian Period persisted from approximately 2112 to 2004 B.C.E., when Babylon defeated Sumer, circa 2000 B.C.E.[29]

Under Babylonian rule, Sumer was a greatly changed place. New deities (often corresponding to Sumerian goddesses and gods) were introduced. The Babylonians learned cuneiform and began to record their history. Several early rulers ordered the transcription of ancient Sumerian texts in an attempt to preserve their wisdom. A collection of such texts (written on clay tablets) was made for the library of Asshurbanipal (668–627 B.C.E.), during a late period of Assyrian rule after this people had conquered Babylon.

Diffuse elements of these cultures were mixed with their Sumerian forerunners. Only with difficulty can we determine which culture created the information contained in the rest of this chapter.

Babylonian and Assyrian Divination

The peoples who inhabited early Babylon seem to have shared much in common with the Sumerians: the will of the deities was absolute, nothing but a dull existence followed death, and the deities had to be constantly propitiated to prevent disastrous calamities.[30] The arts of magic, prophecy, divination, and dream interpretation were fully developed, complete with attendant clergy and specific rites.[31]

The art of divination reached great heights in the Babylonian world as a means of determining the will of the goddesses and gods. The many forms used included *haruspicy* (examination of the livers of sacrificed animals); the observance of omens; *lecanomancy* (determining the signs when oil is poured into water); *libanomancy* (divination by smoke); and other practices.[32] Most of these methods of divination were reserved for use by the clergy, usually for the benefit of the rulers.[33] However, another tool of gaining access to the will of the deities existed—the dream.

Babylonian and Assyrian Dreams

Assyrians recognized that only in sleep could humans freely communicate with the deities.[34] Sometimes this communication took the form of a symbolic dream,[35] but dreams could also be quite clear. Save for those inspired by demons, most dreams were revelations of divine Will.[36]

Babylonian and Assyrian kings heavily relied on dreams to rule their country, to plan and execute the building of public works, to formulate battle plans, and even to lift their spirits. In Her guise as Goddess of War, Ishtar appeared to Asshurbanipal in a dream and directed him to attack a neighboring people.[37]

Later, when the great Assyrian king was feeling disheartened, Ishtar again appeared in a dream and promised that She would march before Asshurbanipal's army and lead it to victory.[38] Another Babylonian king, Nabonidus, saw in a dream Marduk and Sin commanding him to restore the temple at Harran.[39] There are many other examples of such dreams.[40]

During accounts of such spontaneous divine dreams, the deities are often described as "standing at the head" of the sleeper, which may indicate that the deity was believed to enter the dreamer's body through the head.[41] Alternately, the human soul may leave the body and be carried by the deity during sleep.[42]

Dream Incubation

The process of sacred sleep was in more general use in ancient Babylon than it had been in Sumer. There was, however, a major difference: rather than the worshipper receiving the dream, a special class of the diviner clergy (the *shabru*) dreamed for the supplicant.[43]

A special room in the temple was reserved solely for this purpose. Within the room, the *shabru* entered into divine sleep upon the request of the puzzled worshipper. In the morning, the *baru* (diviner) interpreted the dream for the supplicant.[44] Temple sleep (dream incubation) seems to have largely been an emergency measure. Evidence suggests that the more traditional form of dream incubation (in which the supplicant directly receives the divine dream) was also in use,[45] but the "professional sleepers" were quite popular.

At least one example of personal dream incubation has survived, which reveals that relatives or friends could dream for others. When he was in

Babylon, Alexander the Great fell ill. He sent his generals to E-Sagila (the temple of Marduk) to dream a cure for him.[46]

Dream Deities

In common with most other cultures, the Babylonians and Assyrians assigned dreams to specific deities. Among these was the goddess Mamir (also known as Mamu and Mami; She was also a divine midwife) Mamu-da-ge (obviously an emanation of Mamu); Zakar (also spelled Zaqiqu), an emissary of the moon god Sin; and Zakar-mas-ge. Overseeing them all was Shamash, god of the sun, Lord of Vision, the divine creator of dreams. All dream deities were under His control.[47]

Ishtar has already been mentioned as visiting kings in dreams, to lend advice and to relay battle plans. Her fame in this context may be in some way related to Her lunar associations, for as the moon brings light to the darkened nighttime sky, Ishtar brings enlightenment to Her worshippers in the night.

Dream Prayers

Fragments of Assyrian prayers designed to create positive and uplifting dreams (and to prevent evil dreams) have remained. The Assyrian dream prayer below was found in the library of Ashurbanipal:

> *O god of the new moon [Sin];*
> *Unrivaled in might;*
> *Whose counsel no one can grasp;*
> *I have poured for You a pure libation of*
> *   the night,*
> *I have offered You a pure drink,*
> *I bow down to You, I stand before You, I*
> *   seek You!*
> *Direct thoughts of favor and justice*
> *   towards me!*
> *That my god and my goddess who since*
> *   many days have been angry*
> *   towards me,*
> *May be reconciled in right and justice,*
> *   that my path may be fortunate,*
> *   my road straight!*
> *And that He may send Zakar,*
> *   the God of dreams,*
> *   in the middle of the night to*
> *release my sins.*[48]

Dream Interpretation

Assyrian and Babylonian dream interpretation was largely governed by a body of dream material (much of which is now lost). Elements of great importance in dreams included movements, numbers, positions (right or left), and the appearance of deities in the guise of human beings.[49]

In Babylon a series of dream omens named for Zakar (Zaqiqu), the god of dreams,[50] were recorded on eleven tablets. These were probably written in about 1500 B.C.E.[51]

Much is known concerning Assyrian dream interpretation. If the dreamer repeatedly flies, she or he will lose everything,[52] whereas to meet a bird in a dream indicates the future return of a lost belonging.[53] Being given an empty cup foretells future poverty; a full pot, future fame and a large family.[54] Cutting down date trees signifies that the dreamer's problems will be resolved,[55] and seizing a snake indicates divine protection.[56]

Assyrians also accepted the reverse meanings of dreams. Dreaming of being blessed by a deity indicated that deity's wrath against the dreamer, whereas deity-uttered curses against the dreamer meant that her or his prayers would be accepted.[57]

Priestesses of Dream Interpretation

A special class of Akkadian priestesses (*sa'iltu*) were specialists in the interpretation of dreams. These priestesses were found in the earliest times in

Babylonian culture, and were most often consulted by women.[58]

Averting the Influence of Evil Dreams

Some dreams, inspired by the numerous demons that haunted the Babylonian world, were plainly nightmares. Such dreams not only disturbed the person's sleep; they also affected her or his health. When this occurred, the person visited an exorcist to remove the nightmare-causing demon.

Another way to destroy the influence of an evil dream would be to tell the dream to a piece of clay and then dissolve the clay in water while intoning exorcistic prayers. This action freed the dreamer from demon contamination.[59] Similar practices were apparently in use in ancient Sumer.[60]

In a third method used to avert the negative influences of nightmares, the sufferer requested a divine dream that would reveal the most appropriate methods of expelling the evil. Such ritual practices date back to as early as 1700 B.C.E.[61]

Gilgamesh

Dreams play a central role in the *Epic of Gilgamesh*, portions of which date back to ancient Sumer (circa 4000 B.C.E.), though the most complete extant copies are Babylonian. Enkidu, a "wild man" of the forest, has met a courtesan named Shamhat (who was probably a sacred prostitute attached to Ishtar's temple in Uruk).[62] Shamhat tells Enkidu that he must go to Uruk to meet the king, Gilgamesh, a "radiant" man. The courtesan says that Gilgamesh will be notified of Enkidu's approach in his dreams.[63]

Gilgamesh indeed has two prophetic dreams in this epic. In the first, he's walking at night in Uruk with friends when he finds a meteor lying in the street. Gilgamesh tries to lift it but is incapable of doing so because of its weight. Assisted by others, he slings the meteor in thongs and brings it to his mother. Gilgamesh is so attracted to the meteor that, in the dream, he tells his mother, the Goddess Ninsun (worshipped in Uruk and noted for Her wisdom), that the meteor's attraction was like that of a woman. Gilgamesh's mother declares that the meteor is Gilgamesh's brother.[64]

The next morning, Gilgamesh rises and tells his mother of his dream. She explains that the meteor, which She created for him, will be his beloved friend (Enkidu), whom he shall love as a woman, and who will remain faithful to him.[65] Thus,

Shamhat's prediction that Gilgamesh will know of Enkidu's imminent arrival has come true.

Gilgamesh relates to Ninsun a second dream that he has had, in which he was powerfully drawn to a strangely shaped axe that he found lying on the streets of Uruk. He loved the axe as if it were a woman and wore it at his side. His mother interprets the dream by stating that the axe is the brave comrade who is soon to join him in Uruk and rescue his friend.[66]

Thus, Gilgamesh experienced two prophetic dreams, both of which foretold the coming of Enkidu, the wild man of the mountains, who runs naked with the beasts of the hills and sleeps on the ground.

I've dwelled on this epic because it represents one of the earliest Mesopotamian references to prophetic dreams. Since these dreams were sent to Gilgamesh by his mother, the "wise" goddess Ninsun, they can rightly be classified as divinely inspired dreams.

Chapter 4

GREECE

The ancient Greeks are best remembered for their magnificent achievements in art, medicine, political ideals, philosophy, literature, and architecture. They were both original and eclectic, freely borrowing from the peoples of Egypt, Asia Minor, Babylon, and other contemporaneous cultures. Evidence of such cultural borrowing is quite apparent in ancient Greek concepts concerning dreams, which were heavily influenced by Egyptian and Babylonian thought.

TYPES OF DREAMS

The Greeks made a distinction between true and false dreams.[1] They also distinguished between divinely inspired dreams and those that were caused by daily activities and interests.[2] Most dreams were considered to be events that had actually occurred, not as meaningless fantasies.[3]

Pindar stated that, during the day, the soul "slumbered" and the body was active. At night, the body slept and the soul was active, and could receive warnings of the future.[4] During sleep, deities stood at the head of the bed and gave advice to Their worshippers.[5]

Not all Greeks accepted the concept of divine dreams. Democritus wrote that dreams could be emanations from living persons or objects that penetrated the dreamer's consciousness during sleep—a concept that seems to anticipate later theories of telepathy and that denied the divine origin of dreams.[6] The philosopher Xenophanes dismissed all forms of divination, including dreams.[7]

However, most ancient Greek writers (including Plato, Aristotle, Poseidonios, and others) were of the opinion that sleep was a period of communication between humans and divine beings, and that dreams were the memories of such conversations.[8] This concept was widely held throughout the ancient Greek world.

In the earliest times, most divine dreams, Greeks thought, were sent by Zeus. Later, oracular dreams were received from Athena, Hera, Artemis, Asklepios, Hermes (as the emissary of Zeus), Pan (as the "conductor of dreams"), and many other deities. Hermes was especially known as the giver of refreshing sleep, and the god Hypnos specifically ruled sleep.

DREAM INCUBATION

Greek dream incubation (*enkoimisis*), the practice of visiting sacred places with the intention of receiving a useful, inspired dream, was greatly influenced by similar practices of the Egyptians and the Babylonians, though traces of earlier forms of Greek dream incubation are extant. It may have been an established practice well before 333 B.C.E.[9] Dreams received within the sacred precincts of a dream temple were considered to be divinely inspired, more so than those received at home and, thus, were more authoritative.[10]

Some temples were open to anyone desiring a divine dream.[11] Others, including the Greek temples of Isis, would admit only those who had been invited to do so in a dream from the deity.[12] This dream would be recounted to the temple staff, who would ascertain its veracity and determine whether it was a divine call for a temple visit.[13] If a person desiring a divine dream couldn't physically travel to the temple, a relative or a close friend could perform this function in their place.[14]

Dream Incubation Temples

Most of the settings for these temples and sanctuaries were of great natural beauty, far from the cares of everyday life, and the structures themselves were beautiful and of inspiring design. Such temples became so popular that there were 420 dedicated to the dream-healing Asklepios alone,[15] and many were in continuous use for over a thousand years, well into the Hellenic period of Greek history.[16] Visiting a dream temple was one of the most popular religious rites of the time.

Each temple possessed its own practices, which varied from region to region, but all were designed to enhance the probability of divine dreaming and to ensure that such dreams were recalled by the worshipper in the morning.[17]

Upon arrival at the temple, the clergy would determine whether the person was "pure" (ie., free from recent sexual congress). The supplicant was placed on a special diet prohibiting the consumption of certain foods.[18] Alcohol was forbidden also.[19]

Purification ceremonies usually included ritual bathing,[20] anointment with oils,[21] and the burning of frankincense and other fragrant fumigations.[22] The administration of sleep-producing mixtures was also a standard part of pre-incubatory rituals.[23]

The actual ritual usually began with sacrifice (or gifts to the temple) by the supplicant. The nature of this sacrifice or gift was determined by the person's wealth: the poor might offer nothing but flat, thin, perforated cakes dipped in honey or oil, while the wealthier offered money, food, rams,[24] pigs, goats, and other animals.[25]

If a ram had been sacrificed, the worshipper might sleep on or beside the animal's skin.[26] The priests often had a share of the animal sacrifice after it had been "burned" (cooked) on the altar.[27] Animal sacrifice, however, wasn't a prerequisite of dream incubation rituals. Offerings of all kinds were usually accompanied by prayers, chants, and music. Both the supplicant and the temple's clergy prayed for the desired outcome.[28]

Rituals led by the clergy then followed, and may have included leading the supplicants into the temple's inner chamber, to come face-to-face with a large statue of the deity.[29] Sometimes, the diseased part of the worshipper was touched to the statue. Finally, the supplicants dressed in a white garment (thought to induce dreams) and went to sleep in the temple.[30]

Interpretation

By morning, the worshipper may have received a clear dream that needed no interpretation. If this wasn't the case, the temple's clergy interpreted the dream.[31] In healing-dream temples, the nature of the cure provided by the deity (usually Asklepios) was interpreted by the priestesses and priests.[32] Standardized guides to the interpretation of dream symbols were in use in Greece.

NEGATIVE DREAMS

Dreams that were interpreted to foretell future sickness, death, misery, loss of fortune or position, and other negative futures called for action. There were many methods of averting the evil foretold in such a dream. The dream might be recited to Helios (the sun) whose bright light would burn away or frighten the evil. Alternately, sacrifices to protective deities could be made. Minor calamities forecast in dreams were averted by a simple ritual bath.[33]

Dream Incubation and Healing

Although dream temples in very early Greece served many functions, some were associated with healing.[34] A few seem to have been specifically concerned with curing sexual dysfunction and infertility.[35] Following later Egyptian influence, most dream temples became solely concerned with healing.[36]

There were two main forms of dream-directed healing therapies in ancient Greece. The first was dedicated to Asklepios, Who was worshipped in every part of Greece, while the second relied on the theories of Hippocrates.

Asklepios

Asklepios, who lived in about 1100 B.C.E., was described by Homer as a man who had learned the art of medicine from Cheiron, the famous centaur. Over the centuries he was deified and grew to dizzying heights of popularity.

Asklepios' most famed temple was located in Epidaurus. Inscriptions at this temple indicate that His worship began in approximately 500 B.C.E.[37] Stelae uncovered in the ruins of Epidaurus preserve the dreams, diseases, and miraculous cures of many patients who had spent the night at this temple.[38]

Though it was a place of healing and care, no one was allowed to die within the temple's boundaries. Women about to give birth were also forbidden to enter the temple,[39] as the temple had to be kept free from death and birth.[40]

All temples to Asklepios contained impressive statues of the deity. Smaller images of Hypnos (Greek god of sleep), Nyx (god of the night),[41] Hygeia (the goddess who guarded health), and Telesphorus (the god of convalescence) were also present in His temples.[42]

"Thanks" Offerings

A healing would often occur during sleep, at the hands of the temple's attendant deity. These were moments of great celebration and gratitude that demanded the presentation of thanks offerings.[43] Such offerings were made not only to Asklepios, but also to the other attendant deities, including Hygeia, Hypnos, Telesphoros, and others. The sacrifices to Hygeia (as the guardian of health) were considered to be of great importance.[44]

Most of these thanks offerings were of money or sacred objects intended for use in the temple. However, as is the practice at Lourdes today, small models of the healed portions of the worshipper's bodies, made from pottery, ivory, bronze, silver, or gold, were also given.[45]

HIPPOCRATES AND DREAM DIAGNOSIS

Hippocrates (circa 430 B.C.E.) is the alleged author of a large corpus of medical writings. Precisely which of the sixty surviving works (written between 430 and 330 B.C.E.) are by his hand is unclear, for many medical works were attributed to this famous healer. The following references to Hippocrates, then, refer to works by various anonymous authors rather than to books by a single human being.

The Hippocratic tradition of Greek medicine was founded (in part) on the concept that most dreams were useful tools for the diagnosis of disease and other bodily disorders. Hippocrates admitted that some dreams contained divine wisdom, but placed great emphasis on the diagnostic aspect of dreams. He also wrote somewhat disparagingly about Greek dream interpreters, stating that they were at times correct, but that the reverse was often true.[46]

Hippocratic dream lore was quite specific. As with most systems of dream interpretation before Artemidorus (see next page), dream interpretation was standardized. The major distinguishing feature of the Hippocratic method was that most dreams were seen as omens of either impending disease or of future good health. The specific symbols and even the dream's emotional tone were carefully studied.

Positive Hippocratic Dreams

Among the positive dreams that Hippocrates interpreted are included the following: walking "safely" or running swiftly and fearlessly, the sight of rivers flowing smoothly with clear water, and seeing gentle rain and fruit-laden trees.[47] Such dreams indicated that pure living and pure food, air, and water were maintaining the dreamer's health. To see the dead clean of dirt and dressed in white clothing was also considered to be an omen of good health because the dead nourish the living.[48]

Negative Dreams

These were as common as positive omens. If the sight or the hearing was impaired in a dream, this foretold a problem in the head. If rivers ran abnormally, the dreamer was suffering from a blood disorder, a blockage, or some other problem. The dead appearing in a dream naked, dressed in dark clothing, or covered with dirt was a sure sign of disease, as were fighting, stabbing, or being bound.[49]

Hippocrates prescribes prayer for both good and bad dreams. Athena, Zeus, Hermes, and Apollo were thanked for positive dreams, while negative dreams were times for prayer to the Heroes (including Heracles), Gaea, and to all deities that averted evil influences, including Zeus.[50]

ARTEMIDORUS AND DREAM INTERPRETATION

In about 140 B.C.E., a Lydian named Artemidorus wrote his epic work: a five-volume guide to dream interpretation titled the *Oneirocritica* (*The Interpretation of Dreams*). He had been inspired in a dream from Apollo to take on this enormous task, and it was quite successful. The *Oneirocritica* is the most complete work of dream interpretation to have survived from the ancient world.

Artemidorus' task was simple, yet revolutionary. He set out to separate the superstitious elements of dream interpretation (ie., those not based on fact) from the proven methods.[51] Of even greater importance was his concept that the dreamer's individuality had to be taken into account to accurately interpret a dream.[52]

Artemidorus wrote that dreams reveal the future and that they could be invaluable guides for human action. Artemidorus based his attitude and theories on historical fact, oral tradition, and personal experience.[53] He thought that dreams were "infused" in humans for their advantage and instruction. Though he hesitated to state the dreams came directly from deities,[54] many of them held important messages for their dreamers and thus should be carefully interpreted.

Artemidorus agreed that there were many types of dreams, including those that predicted the future or that possessed some other importance, and those that were merely reflections of daily life (in sleep, the hungry person eats, the thirsty one drinks, the lover sees her or his sweetheart).[55] Only prophetic dreams were deserving of interpretation, and Artemidorus created a plan of such relevance and logic that it actually enjoyed its greatest popularity in the seventeenth and eighteenth centuries (see Chapter 8).

Artemidorus' works were written for everyone interested in the interpretation of dreams, and specifically for professional dream interpreters, who were common in ancient Greece.

Artemidorus' Instructions for Dream Interpreters

The interpreter questions the dreamer regarding her or his personal life and other factors that might affect the dream's meaning. Artemidorus stated that it was vital to know the dreamer's name, occupation, date of birth, state of health, wealth, and marital status.[56]

Taking into consideration the above information, the interpretation began. Artemidorus' extensive lists of dream meanings would be consulted—keeping in mind the above factors. Search would be made for puns or other forms of word-play.[57] (This last technique was probably borrowed from ancient Egyptian dream interpretation.) From this involved process, the interpreter slowly pieced together the dream's message.

Artemidorus' method was an extraordinary development in the history of dream interpretation. For the first time, dreams were seen as singular experiences. intimately related to those who received them, and incapable of being solely interpreted by reference to dusty lists. The age of modern dream interpretation had been born. True, most of the interpretation was performed by professionals and not by the dreamers themselves, but the way had been paved for the dream books that are published today.

Dream Interpretations from Artemidorus

Artemidorus' lists of dream symbols are exhaustive. These include the parts of the body, animals, plants, insects, foods and liquids, occupations, drugs, various forms of sexual activity, birth, and virtually every aspect of life. Though he provided lists of dreams and their possible meanings, Artemidorus took great pains to include a variety of meanings, for the same dream, for persons of various professions, social position, marital status, even religious orientation.

Dreaming that one's head has been shaved is unfortunate to anyone but a priest of Isis, for whom it is a positive sign. For sailors, it presages shipwreck; for the ill, a further collapse in health (but not death). Artemidorus states his rationale: those who have been shipwrecked, and persons who recover from serious illnesses, are shaved; the dead are not.[58]

Some other dreams from Artemidorus include: dreaming of being anointed with oils is highly favorable for women (except adulteresses); of being sick, auspicious for those in captivity or for the ill; of drinking cold water, good fortune; of drinking hot water, failure or future disease.[59]

Artemidorus' fifth volume contained ninety-five actual dreams, their interpretations, and their manifestations. In one, a man in exile (in poor financial position) dreamed that his mother twice gave birth to him. He returned to his "motherland" to find that his mother was ill. He soon inherited her property. A woman once dreamed that her lover had presented her with the head of a pig. After this dream, she soon broke off the relationship, for Aphrodite doesn't favor pig's heads. One man dreamed that an olive tree was growing from his head and developed wisdom and eloquence that approached even that of the goddess represented by the olive, the wise Athena.[60]

SEEING DEITIES IN DREAMS

Though Artemidorus skirted the issue of whether or not all dreams were actually sent by deities, he states that deities could appear in dreams and, by their very presence, predict the dreamer's positive or negative future. The goddesses and gods themselves didn't reveal messages in words; their presences alone were sufficient.[61]

It was of little importance whether the deity appeared as a living being or in the form usually seen in statuary, save that, when seen as living persons, the dream message would more quickly come to fruition.[62]

The following list of deities seen in dreams and their omens has been compiled from Book 2 of Artemidorus' *Oneirocritica:*

Aesculapius: Seen on a pedestal and adored, good luck. Seeing Him moving, approaching, or entering a house: for the healthy, sickness or famine; for the sick, recovery.

Apollo: Favorable to musicians, prophets, physicians, and philosophers. For all: secrets will be revealed; possible travel.

Artemis: For those who fear, good fortune, for She will protect them. For pregnant women, highly auspicious. For hunters and fishers, good fortune. For all: the finding of lost articles. Seeing Artemis nude is highly inauspicious for all persons.

Athena: Positive for those who work with handicrafts, for farmers and philosophers. For unmarried men, a positive future marriage. For courtesans, an unfavorable future.

Demeter: To those initiates of Demeter's mysteries, an incredibly fortunate occurrence in the future. To the sick, recovery. To all others, fear and danger, eventuating in great accomplishments.

Dionysius: Auspicious for innkeepers; farmers who cultivate vines and fruit trees, and all those in difficulty. To the wealthy and to children, danger, scandal, plots, and distur-bances, which He will avert.

Hecate: Seen as three-faced, standing on a pedestal. Favorable: signifies foreign travel. The presence of Hecate in a dream also indicates the impossibility for the dreamer to remain in the same circumstances; great change is approaching. Artemidorus adds that it is dangerous and unwise to write further concerning Hecate's appearance in a dream, and directs the interested reader to one of Her initiates for more information.

Hera: For wealthy and influential women, a favorable future. Of less significance to men who see Her in their dreams.

Hermes: Favorable for orators, gymnastic instructors, athletes, traders, and business persons. To the sick, death.

Iris: (Usually seen in dreams as a rainbow.) Generally favorable for the very poor or those experiencing difficulties, for the future will shift in their favor. If seen on the right, a positive future. If on the left, negative. (This orientation is based on the position of the rainbow in relation to the sun, not on the dreamer's location.)

Pan: Favorable for shepherds (and, possibly, theatrical performers). To all others, confusion and shaky futures.

Persephone: Good luck for those who live in fear, for the poor, for the workers of arcane magic and mystic rites. However, threatening actions by the goddess in a dream reveal an inauspicious future.

Selene: (Seen as the moon in dreams.) Favorable for business persons and navigators.

Zeus: For the wealthy and powerful, good fortune; for the sick, healing. Seeing Him seated is favorable; moving to the east, auspicious; toward the west, inauspicious.[63]

In *The Republic*, Plato wrote that, during sleep, humans enjoy a special hold on truth. The extensive use of dreams for diagnosis, healing, glimpses of the future, and for other purposes in ancient Greece seems proof enough that this culture paid heed to such sacred truths.

Chapter 5

ROME

A ncient Rome was a curiously cosmopolitan place. At various times during its history, deities from Egypt, Greece, Persia, and certain other Mediterranean countries were honored in the Roman Empire. At first, in Rome, much of this worship was performed in secret.[1] However, when the emperor Caracalla removed all legal bans on the worship of foreign deities, the religious character of Rome was quickly and dramatically changed.[2]

The acceptance of foreign deities in Rome soon spread their worship throughout the Roman Empire. Isis is an excellent example. The Egyptian goddess was first introduced into Rome from Greece. Soon, temples, shrines, and sanctuaries to Isis were in use in Great Britain, France (Gaul), Germany, Switzerland, Spain, Cyprus, the Cycladic Islands, the Balearic Islands, and along much of the northern coast of Africa—in virtually every country that had fallen before the sword of Rome.

DREAMS

Much of what has been said concerning dreams and Greece equally applies to Rome. One researcher writes that Romans were addicted to all forms of divination,[3] and this extended to the interpretation of dreams.

Some dreams were inspired by the divinities. Temple incubation was in wide use. The importance that ancient Romans gave to dreams can be demonstrated by a law proclaimed by the emperor Augustus. The law stated that anyone who had a dream concerning Rome was required to relate it publicly in the marketplace, just in case it contained a divine warning for the emperor or the commonwealth.[4]

Dreams were popular sources of information for all classes of society. The emperors Tiberius and Caligula both foresaw their own deaths in dreams.[5] The poet Philemon, while asleep one night, dreamed of seeing nine young women leaving his house. He recounted this dream to his boy, finished the play that he'd been writing, and went back to sleep. He was dead within hours. The nine women he had seen were obviously the Muses, Who were leaving his home so as not to be polluted by the negative energies of death.[6]

Pliny the Elder, who rejected most popular religious and magical rites, wholeheartedly accepted the wisdom of dreams. He was directed in a dream to write an account of the Roman/German wars.[7] In his *Natural History*, Pliny records that the cure for hydrophobia (the root of the wild rose) was revealed to a woman in a dream, who then asked her son to obtain this medicine.[8] He also interpreted the disturbing dreams of his friend Suetonius.[9]

Conflicting Ideas Concerning Dreams

As was the case in Greece, some writers divorced themselves from the concept that the deities could send dreams to their worshippers, or that the dreams bore any hidden meanings. "Let this divination of dreams be rejected with the rest," Cicero wrote.[10] Titus Lucretius stated that dreams were nothing more than nighttime visions of waking events and sights.[11] Philosophers, however, were notorious for attempting to divorce themselves from the popular religious attitudes of their times, so we can't assume that such beliefs were widespread.

Galen, the great physician who spent much of his time attacking the superstitious activities of the Romans, had somewhat ambivalent ideas concerning the power of dreams. When he was seventeen, he had a dream that convinced him to turn his back on philosophy, in favor of studying medicine. Though he didn't believe that disease could be diagnosed from dreams, he wrote that dreams often led him to effective treatments.[12]

Most Romans, however, saw dreams as divine messages. Dream oracular temples had been in use since the earliest days of Rome, but their popularity increased one-hundred-fold when worship of the Greek god Asklepios was officially introduced to Rome.

When a severe plague swept Rome in 293 B.C.E., Aesculapius (the Roman spelling of Asklepios) was petitioned to end it. His worship in Rome began that year, and by January, 291 B.C.E., His temple on the Insula Tiberina was formally dedicated.[13] Aesculapius' temples were soon found in every part of the Roman Empire.

Dream Incubation

Roman dream incubation closely resembled Greek practices. The inspiring temples built for this use were situated near springs and rivers, and their primary (though not only) function lay in the diagnosis and treatment of illness. The familiar procedures were followed: visitation of the temple; purification, offerings or sacrifices, prayer, sleep, interpretation, diagnosis, and—when appropriate—prescriptions for cures. A special class of temple employees, known as the *necori*, were the dream interpreters. The necori may have also been physicians.[14]

Dream Deities

Before the spread of foreign dream deities, Rome honored several native goddesses and gods Who performed similar functions. Of these, perhaps Fauna (or Faula) and Faunus are of most interest.

Fauna was an ancient Italic agricultural goddess, a personification of the rich, fertile earth. She was worshipped by women and was highly regarded as a giver of dream oracles.[15] Fauna was also the bestower of health.[16]

Variously described as the sister or "wife" of Faunus (see below), Her worship became associated with that of Ops, Terra, and Bona Dea. Bona Dea (literally, "the Good Goddess") became so closely associated with Fauna that She was eventually known as the Good Goddess.[17]

Faunus was an old Roman god, equally connected with agriculture, as well as with pastures, woodlands, and shepherds. His worshippers seem to have been limited to men only, especially farmers who asked Faunus to bless their crops. He also sent dream messages to His worshippers.[18]

Among the foreign deities that offered oracular dreams, none was as popular as Isis. An early Isian temple was established at Piraeus in Greece by the fourth century B.C.E.,[19] and Isis slowly made Her way into Rome. Though Her temples were periodically destroyed by imperial decree, the worship of Isis in ancient Rome soon became a widespread institution. Part of Isis' appeal was Her practice of providing advice and healings in dreams. From the days of Cicero, the Isian dream oracles were famous throughout the Roman world.

Diodorus writes that Her priestesses and priests could recount the innumerable healings that Isis had bestowed on Her worshippers in Her dream temples.[20] Indeed, one of the reasons for Isis' great popularity is that actual healings seem to have also occurred during sacred sleep within Her temples.[21]

Serapis also enjoyed wide popularity. A temple to Serapis in Rome had been established as early as 150 B.C.E.,[22] and His worship grew in concert with that of Isis. Indeed, temples to Isis and Serapis were often built side by side. Serapis was particularly noted for providing oracular and healing dreams. His worship was outshone only by the devotion paid to Isis.

The End of Roman Dream Incubation

Rome's willingness to embrace the worship of foreign deities was eventually responsible for the darkest period in Western European history. Only one deity was necessary to create this catastrophe. After the official Roman acceptance of Christianity, bathing was soon considered to be "Pagan," and thus was a largely forbidden practice. Sewage systems were left in disrepair (for the goddess of the sewers, Cloacina, was no longer worshipped). The rich scientific knowledge of Egypt, Babylon, and Greece was ignored due to its links with Pagan deities and practices. Rome's eagerness to adopt the sole worship of yet another foreign god led to the endless, horrifying centuries of the Dark Ages.

Over a thousand years would pass before Europeans pulled the veil of sleep from their eyes. They finally began studying the classical authors and eventually launched a new era of scientific thought. Even then, scientists were constantly warned by the Church not to produce discoveries that questioned Biblical veracity.

The official conversion of the Roman Empire to Christianity temporarily halted the ancient methods of dream incubation (and all other ritual practices). However, every Roman didn't become a Christian overnight. The dream-healing temples were so popular and numerous that the worship of their deities (Asklepios, Isis, and Serapis) were among the last Pagan practices to be eliminated during the early Roman Christian era. Indeed, it was only through intense persecution that the worship of Isis in Rome was finally (at least officially) abolished.

When most traces of Pagan worship had been stamped out, the early Christian church began its infamous process of converting earlier practices to acceptable Christian forms. Forms of dream incubation were permitted, but only in churches dedicated to the Christian God.[23] Fasting was allowed as a means of producing such dreams. Eventually, Christian temple sleep was transformed into an idealized human quest for divine inspiration.[24]

The long history of European and Middle Eastern ritual dream practices was coming to a close. The political triumph of Christian ideals not only destroyed the concept of personal religion, it also robbed us of direct communication with our deities. Sacred sleep was forgotten. Goddesses and gods languished in their divine realms. Humans marched toward technological madness built upon the new religion's belief that the Earth, far from being sacred, was an object deserving to be plundered and exploited to our fullest capabilities.

Chapter 5

Though humanity remained curious about dreams, they had forgotten the most important of their many sources: the divinities who watch over us in the night.

Chapter 6

HAWAI'I

The fertile islands of the Hawaiian archipel-
ago supported the development of a remarkable culture. Geographic isolation fostered
total independence. Agriculture, astronomy,
medicine, and navigation reached the pinnacles
of achievement.

In common with most Polynesian cultures,
the ancient Hawaiians were a deeply spiritual
people. Rain, wind, snow, vulcanism, mists, mi-
rages, plants, trees, birds, fish, sharks, animals,
and stones were recognized as "bodies" of the

deities. The deities weren't invented to explain natural forces and processes; Their presences were discovered within those processes. Hawaiian religion was based on personal experience and communication with these deities.[1]

A multitude of goddesses and gods received worship in the form of island-wide rituals, local rites, secret ceremonies, daily home rituals, rites for deities of specific crafts and occupations, and private acts of faith. Among the deities so honored were Kane, giver of sunlight and fresh water; Haumea, the mother goddess Who presided over childbirth; Hina, goddess of the moon, of forests and the sea, Who was invoked while gathering medicinal plants; Ku, the male generative force; Laka, goddess of the hula; Lono, god of agriculture, rain, peace, fertility, and the provider of food, and, of course, Pele, goddess of volcanos, vulcanism, and fire in all its forms, Who continues to be openly worshipped today. Every aspect of life was infused with spirituality.

THE KAHUNA

The once-noble role of the *kahuna* (expert) of Hawaiʻi has been grossly distorted by biased and misinformed Western interpreters. *Kahuna* weren't sorcerers. They weren't frightening creatures. They were experts in various fields: herbal medicine, bone-setting, massage, architecture, surfing, athletics, agriculture, midwifery, astronomy, meteorology, navigation, carving, bird catching, and dance, among other disciplines. Though female kahuna were uncommon, some women did attain this status.

Some kahuna were religious experts, attached to *heiau* (temples). They performed spiritual rituals and oversaw the periodic maintenance of the temple's wooden structures. Others specialized in magic, including divination, exorcism, the observation of omens, and love rituals of many types.

Training in all kahuna specialties was intense and required years of concentrated observation and study. The student wasn't expected to ask questions, but to learn by observation. Training in just one field often required twenty years of intense study, governed by strict *kapu* (taboos).

Chapter 6

THE END OF TRADITIONAL
HAWAIIAN CULTURE

Traditional Hawaiian religion and culture officially collapsed in 1819. Captain James Cook landed at Kealakekua Bay on the island of Hawai'i on Monday, January 19, 1778 C.E. Soon afterward, foreign ships began dropping anchor in the aquamarine waters off the islands in search of provisions and entertainment. Exposure to Western customs gradually eroded popular acceptance of the ancient faith. Women were also becoming dissatisfied with the stringent religious and social taboos placed upon their activities.

In an incredible coincidence, the first missionaries from Boston arrived the following year (1820), just after traditional Hawaiian religion (with its attendant calendar and taboos) had been officially abolished by King Liholiho and his chief kahuna, Hewahewa. Ka'ahumanu, the powerful widow of Kamehameha II, also had a hand in destroying the faith—she had taken an interest in Christianity. Thus, the end of traditional Hawaiian religion came, not at the hands of the missionaries, but through the actions of the culturally adrift Hawaiians, themselves.

Temples were abandoned (some priests had to be forced from them). Thousands of intricately carved *ki'i* (wooden images of the deities) were destroyed. Still, many secretly clung to the old faith. These women and men would meet under spreading trees to listen to the endless sermons of the missionaries (presented in a mixture of Hawaiian and Tahitian), then would catch a fish to use in love magic.

Because the Hawaiians lacked an alphabet, much of their ancient culture has been lost. There are no Hawaiian equivalents of the library of Ashurbanipal, no baked clay tablets, no old papyri; but fortunately, some aspects of traditional spiritual information were recorded in books and newspapers by both foreigners and Hawaiians soon after the arrival of the first missionaries.

Other lore was retained in the memories of those who had lived before the days of acculturation. This knowledge was passed on to succeeding generations, and portions of it were recorded in the first half of this century by anthropologists and sociologists. Today, most of the truly learned experts have long since entered *po* (night; the underworld).

Traditional Hawaiian culture has been officially dead for less than 200 years, but from its remaining lore we can gain an accurate picture of the place of dreams in their society.

HAWAIIAN DREAMING

The importance of dreams in traditional Hawaiian culture cannot be overstated. Dreams were memories of nighttime communications with the *'aumakua* (deified ancestral spirits) and the *akua* (goddesses and gods). Dream interpretation was a serious art, for dreams represented communications between the human world and the realm of the deities.[2]

The Hawaiians termed the human soul the *'uhane*. Dreams were known as *moe 'uhane* (literally, "soul sleep"). During sleep, the immortal human soul left the body through the *lua 'uhane* ("spirit pit"), the tear duct located at the inner corner of the eye.

The human soul wandered about, either in this world or in other realms, and had many adventures: visiting distant locations or other islands, meeting with both familiar and strange human souls, and having other interesting experiences. Dreams, then, are the remembrances of the *'uhane's* experiences and travels during sleep.[3]

It is in this physically detached state that the 'uhane met with her or his 'aumakua (deified ancestral spirits) and the akua (goddesses and gods). Divine messages were often communicated in such meetings. At dawn, or when tired of traveling, the soul re-entered the human body through the lua 'uhane, and the dreamer soon awoke.[4]

Dreams, then, could either be messages from divinities, or remembrances of the soul's adventures while traveling in the night. Hawaiians often began a recitation of dreams with the words, "My spirit saw . . ."[5] rather than "I had the strangest dream."

Danger in the Night

The sleeping human body was susceptible to possession by spirits. Mischievous spirits (there are ritual references to over 400,000 goddesses, gods, spirits, and semi-divine beings) could enter the body, creating dreams of nightmarish quality. Some spirits had sex with the sleeping person and half-human babies were occasionally produced from these unions. These spirits could be either female (*wahine o ka po*, "wife of the night") or male (*kane o ka po*, "husband of the night").[6]

All negative dreams demanded immediate action. The dreamer prayed to the deities for protection from the foretold danger, or, at the least, for them to "sweeten" the future (ie., to reduce the impending disaster). Additionally, the deity may have been invoked to "sever" (*oki*) the unpleasant future.[7] The rationale was that, because the deity had sent the dream (and was planning to punish Her or His worshipper), She or He could certainly be supplicated for mercy.[8] Such prayers to "sweeten" dreams are still in use in Hawai'i.[9]

Sacred Sleep in Hawai'i

Hawaiians also practiced what could be termed dream incubation, though the techniques differed from those found in the ancient world. It wasn't necessary to visit a temple; the technique could be performed at home. The origins of this practice are difficult to determine. It is possible that the concept accompanied the Polynesians when they left Asia and began settling the thousands of islands that dot the vast Pacific Ocean. (Many aspects of Hawaiian culture are markedly Asian in flavor.) Alternately, the practice of asking for dreams may have been a local development on Hawai'i, a natural invention by an intensely spiritual people.

Hawaiian medical kahuna were highly skilled individuals, representing a great number of medical specialties. Occasionally, however, a case puzzled *kahuna haha* (diagnostician), a *kahuna la'au lapa'au* (medicinal herbalist), or some other medical expert.

When this occurred, the kahuna told the patient to return for treatment on the following day. That night, while the expert slept (usually in the healing temple), the kahuna's deity appeared in a dream and provided the appropriate diagnosis or treatment (sea baths, steam baths, enemas, medicinal mixtures, specialized diets). Upon awakening, this information would be quite clear in the kahuna's mind.[10]

Dream incubation was also practiced at home. When problems or questions arose (sickness, new ventures, questions concerning distant relatives), the head of the household (virtually always a man) prayed in the *mua* (the men's eating house, generally forbidden to women) and spent the night there. In his sleep, the family's deity would appear and provide the appropriate information.[11]

Information Unexpectedly Received in Dreams

Persons who were ill frequently received remedies for their conditions in dreams. Such prescriptions were quite exacting and usually included the location in which the materials could be found. Many of these prescriptions that had come "in the night" were passed to others and became an established part of Hawaiian folk medicine.[12]

The provider of this information may have been a long-deceased (and deified) ancestor, an unknown personage, or even a disembodied voice. These dream remedies were precise: two handfuls of an herb, four buds from a plant, three baths. Such informational dreams have persisted to this day.[13]

Information of all types could unexpectedly be delivered in dreams. Songs and even dance movements for the *hula* were often received,[14] usually from deceased relatives. Fishermen might dream of the most productive area of the ocean in which to work.

Even names were received in dreams. During a woman's pregnancy, the woman herself, or a family member, was sometimes given a name for the child in a dream. Such names (*inoa po*; literally, "night names") were provided by ancestral deities as well as by the gods themselves. Failure to give this name to the child could prove dangerous to the baby. The deity that had bestowed the name would be the future child's divine guardian.[15]

The Nature of Hawaiian Dreams

Our culture tends to think of dreams as being largely visual. We speak of having "seen" this or that in our dreams. Hawaiians, however, could have purely visual dreams, purely auditory dreams (in which disembodied voices were heard), or a combination of both. Auditory dreams seem to have been as common as visual dreams.[16] Their messages were obvious and direct, and hardly needed interpretation. The voices heard were those of deities.

Most Hawaiian dreams were concerned with the sleeper's family, friends, profession, and other immediate concerns. Dreams of traveling to exotic locales or to spiritual places were virtually unknown. Dreams clearly reflected the everyday lives and concerns of their dreamers.[17]

Hawaiian dream prophecies weren't always connected with the dreamer, for sleepers could dream for others (usually family members).[18] Dreams were of such importance to the Hawaiians that a negative dream about a relative was always followed by a visit to the person, to warn her or him of the prophecy.[19]

Dream Interpretation

Dream interpretation was an important part of ancient Hawaiian culture. This function wasn't performed by clergy in temples but by a family member or a close friend. Many families had a *wehewehe moe 'uhane* (dream interpreter). Since Hawaiians often dreamed for family members, all important dreams were carefully discussed each morning by the entire family.

Many dreams required no interpretation. When the dreamer awoke, the message was quite clear. Such dreams were termed *moe pi'i pololei*. These were usually predictive in nature.[20]

Only those dreams that were symbolically complex, confusing, or worrisome were interpreted. Dream interpretations (*moe kuluma*) weren't standardized as they were in the ancient world. Though some dream interpretations seem to have been widely accepted, each region of each island and every family possessed its own set of interpretations.[21]

Interpretation began by examining the dream's major symbols (sharks, nudity, spilling water, and so on). Next, the interpreter took into account the dreamer's individuality (as a relative or a close friend, the dreamer was known to the interpreter) and determined whether the dream was of any significance.[22]

Many seemingly negative dream symbols were interpreted as being positive. The reverse was also true. Dreaming of death never indicated impending death;[23] death symbols were always far subtler than this. In common with the ancient Egyptians, Greeks, Assyrians, Romans, and Sigmund Freud, Hawaiians knew that dreams often bore reverse meanings.[24]

A few traditional dream symbols and their interpretations have been recorded. Many were in use only among certain families, but some were Hawaiian cultural symbols and bore meanings for far larger sectors of the population.

Bananas: Dreaming of bananas signified that to go fishing in the morning would be useless—no fish would be caught.[25] This interpretation is still accepted by many cultural Hawaiians.

Cave: An omen of death. (Bodies were placed in caves in old Hawai'i.)[26]

Canoe: To see a canoe in a dream foretold bad luck on the following day.[27] It also predicted the death of someone known to the dreamer.[28] (Bodies were sometimes placed in canoes; hence, the death symbolism.)

Dead, the: To dream of seeing the dead indicated either the imminent arrival of food, or that someone among the living wished to see the dreamer.[29]

Human genitals: Seen in a dream, they were omens of impending disappointment.[30]

Tooth, losing a: This indicated that a relative would soon die.[31]

Water: Dreaming of seeing clear water was a positive sign.[32]

Dreams and the messages that they often contained were of the greatest importance to the Hawaiians. They were sources of information, counselling, warning, healing, protection, professional advice, and omens of the future. Lacking books, Hawaiians turned to the largest repository of knowledge that was available to them: the combined wisdom and experiences of the goddesses and gods, sent "out of the night" through the form of dreams.

Chapter 7

North America

Well over one million persons were living in North America when the first known Europeans landed on its shores. A great diversity of cultures flourished in most parts of the continent, from the swamps of the south to the great midwestern plains; the mountains and the buttes; the tall timber country and deserts. Though some of these cultures were linguistically or otherwise related, most possessed unique religions, languages, and customs.

A few centuries later, the indigenous population had been decimated by disease, war, and slavery. Many cultures died out—the only traces of their existence the artifacts found during excavations at their ancient living sites.

The history of European interaction with Native Americans is a study in greed, exploitation, subjugation, cruelty, and, finally, indifference. Explorations continued and settlements were established, forcing the indigenous population into the least-valued areas of the continent. The Europeans felt that they had a divine right to live on the continent, and that the original inhabitants did not. Native Americans were treated with disdain as devil-worshipping idiots; their rich cultures as meaningless mumbo-jumbo. As the Spanish forcibly introduced Catholicism, many aspects of traditional Native American traditions were forever lost.

The story of European interaction with the indigenous population of North America represents one of the darkest periods of our continent's history. Only our acceptance and support of slavery equals its cruelty.

Fortunately, some aspects of Native American cultures have survived. As early as the 1600s, Jesuit priests recorded the spiritual practices of the Iroquois. In the late 1800s and early 1900s, many anthropologists spent much time speaking to elderly Native American informants, recording medicinal lore, languages, family structure, clothing, games, methods of food gathering, agriculture, and religious beliefs. A few acculturated Native Americans even wrote autobiographies.

Surveying the range of material that was collected, it becomes apparent that few generalizations can be made concerning the religious practices of Native Americans. The great diversity of sacred stories ("myths"), songs, dances, and ritual practices reflected each culture's unique world-view and location on this huge continent.

One of the few common elements in most Native American cultures was the significance placed on dreams. The methods in which dreams related to waking life substantially differed among various peoples, but dreams played an important role in most of these societies.

It was widely believed that dreams were sent by divinities or spirits, but some cultures thought of them as rising from the dreamer's soul. Dreams were also ritually produced by fasting, sleeping in wild places, or through the ingestion of vegetable drugs (during puberty rites as well as on other occasions). Dreams revealed songs, dances, patterns for handicrafts, and medicinal cures; they lent spiritual power to the dreamer and were a major source of information and education. Dreams were necessary to attain certain societal roles (midwife, shaman, shamaness) and often predicted future events.

A lengthier synthesis of Native American dream lore would be a useless exercise in generalization. Hence, this chapter individually explores the importance of dreams within a few groups.

Because the following information was recorded by Europeans after the time of Western contact, some of this lore may not be truly representative of Native American peoples' earlier practices and concepts. The Eurocentric, patriarchal bias of the male collectors must also be taken into account. This certainly explains the dearth of material relating specifically to women.

Additionally, most Native American cultures didn't live together in large numbers. They were scattered in small communities over large areas of land. Local landmarks, weather, and cultural distance led to a certain variety in each community's spiritual practices and concepts. Thus, even the following information should not be perceived as representative of every community of the group.

NAVAJO

The Navajo placed great importance on dreams. It is possible that their entire understanding of divinity (spirits) as well as their methods of contacting them (religious ritual) were originally culled from dreams.[1]

Dreams were either positive or negative.[2] Negative dreams demanded a serious course of action, including both personal and community rituals.[3] Both positive and negative dreams could be "placed in the head" of the dreamer by deities, spirits, and animals.[4]

One Navajo shaman's attitudes toward dreams were recorded in 1932. White Hair stated that every dream that he had ever experienced had manifested in his life. Dreams are not silly fantasies; they are prophetic of either current or future events. White Hair also stated that humans of all nations were created to dream.[5]

Some dreams were considered to be the cause (not the revelation) of ill health. A dream of this nature led the dreamer to a diagnostician, who would find the sickness' origin and set a cure into motion. Less threatening sicknesses could be treated by the dreamer praying at dawn at her or his doorway, sometimes with a stone that had been specially empowered by the diagnostician for this purpose. More serious dream-caused sicknesses demanded extensive ceremonies led by shamans,[6] including the famous sandpainting rituals.[7] Specific rituals and chants were required for specific types of negative dreams.[8] These curing rituals were also revealed in dreams. Since disease was created by evil magicians, spirits, and the dead, appropriate magical measures were used to combat these conditions.[9] If, during a curing ritual of several days' length, the shaman dreamed that the patient had died, he would leave the rite to be replaced by another shaman.[10]

Some Navajo dreams (those regarding snakes, owls, and bears) possessed standardized interpretations that seemed to have been widely accepted.[11] Dreams of snakes were positive (unless the snake bit), and teeth being pulled predicted a death in the family.[12]

Pregnant Navajo women were especially wary of any dream that contained violence or altercations, for the effects of such dreams could harm their unborn children. The dream's evil influence was averted by rituals during the woman's pregnancy.[13]

Less information is recorded concerning positive dreams among the Navajo; they seem to have been regarded as rather rare occurrences. However, we do know that to ensure that a positive dream occurred, the dreamer could consult a shaman to "sing" for the dream to come to fruition, or she or he could simply sprinkle corn meal about and pray that the fortunate dream came true.[14]

OJIBWA (CHIPPEWA)

The Ojibwa classified dreams in the following categories: bad, good, beautiful,[15] impure, ominous, unlucky, and painful. They saw dreams as a major source of education. Teaching occurred during sleep and the instructors were the deities (spirits). Whatever wisdom or knowledge a human possessed was the direct result of dreams. Courage, healing abilities, creativity, bravery, and all other valued human attributes were the direct result of dreams.[16]

Ojibwa boys, upon reaching puberty, fasted for four days in solitude to prepare themselves to receive a dream song of great power. All children were encouraged to dream as well as to remember their dreams from an early age.[17]

We know something about the role that dreams played in Ojibwa women's lives. They, too, received wisdom and knowledge from the spirits in dreams.[18] Midwives (all of whom were women) were often called to their profession by dreams, as childbirth dreams endowed a woman with the power to facilitate this process in other women. Dream symbols related to midwifery included animals who easily delivered their young, such as female dogs, mares, or cows. At times, the animal would speak to the dreamer and promise to assist her during childbirth. Not surprisingly, midwives were held in high esteem in ancient Ojibwa society.[19]

The Ojibwa (in common with the Northern Algonquin and the Northern Athabaskans) interpreted some dreams as signs of reincarnation. They found the proof of this in dreams that concerned events from other lives—events that had not occurred during the dreamer's present life.[20]

One young man of the Parry Island Ojibwa (near Port Huron) experienced a dream that concerned a grave containing a valuable object. The grave was dug and a gun was discovered within it. The man's tribe immediately proclaimed that he was the reincarnation of the warrior who had been buried a century earlier in that grave.[21]

IROQUOIS

A clue as to the significance of dreams to the Iroquois can be found in the writings of the seventeenth-century Jesuit missionary Pere Fremin, who wrote that the Iroquois thought and talked of nothing else.[22] They shared their dreams with everyone who would listen.

To the Iroquois, the dream state was of greater importance than waking consciousness, precisely the opposite of our society's materialistic view.[23] Some Europeans misunderstood this to mean that the Iroquois were incapable of differentiating between dream states and waking states. This was erroneous, for the Iroquois more highly valued the dream state; therefore, they were well able to distinguish the two.

The Iroquois seem to have comprehended the existence of the two minds: the conscious and the subconscious.[24] The "soul" was apparently the subconscious mind, and was at work during sleep.

They also recognized two types of dreams: *personal* (dreams that detailed the soul's unfulfilled wishes) and *visitation* (in which spiritual beings appeared to the dreamer and imparted messages of great significance for both the dreamer and her or his entire community).[25]

Personal dreams were seen as messages of the soul's frustrated wishes. The soul was unable to communicate with the conscious mind during waking hours. Therefore, these wishes were sent to the conscious mind in the form of dreams. This is virtually identical to Freud's theory, yet the Iroquois recognized it hundreds of years earlier.

To determine the exact nature of the soul's wishes, personal dreams were interpreted by the dreamer, a specialized dream interpreter, or a diviner. A process similar to free association seems to have been used that approached modern psychoanalytic practice.[26] Divination was also used to gain an understanding of personal dreams. The interpreter placed an herb under her or his head and slept on it to obtain a clarifying dream, or gazed into water (in a method similar to crystal-gazing) to find the answer. Both women and men served as dream interpreters, and some attained high social positions.[27]

Once the soul's wishes were known, they were seriously considered. To soothe the tormented soul, the personal dream was either physically enacted or ritualistically performed, in private or in concert with the entire community.[28] To avoid acting out the messages contained in dreams could bring harm to the dreamer as well as to the community.[29]

Even personal dreams of seemingly little importance were symbolically or actually enacted.[30] Visitation dreams were of tremendous impact. In them, the dreamer was visited in the night by a deity or spirit. These dreams may have included advice (such as assuming a new societal role), comfort, or warnings of the future. Others were concerned with community affairs.[31] Some of these visitation dreams were clear and explicit; others had to be interpreted.[32]

In common with many other Native American groups, Iroquois shamans were chosen on the basis of dreams.[33]

Chapter 7

Maricopa

The Maricopa saw success or skill in physical life as the result of spiritual activities that occurred during sleep. At night, the dreamer's soul wandered in search of a divine being who would reveal the necessary information. All success in life was the product of these nighttime encounters.[34]

Such dreams were created through a long ritual process that was fraught with both difficulty and danger. The information obtained in this fashion might be doled out in small portions over many years, the "spirit" (deity) appearing each evening and furthering the student's education. Dreams of this nature, and the information contained within them, were kept secret until the student had gained a proper understanding of the material. Speaking of these lessons before wisdom and insight had been attained would anger the deity, causing her or him to abandon the dreamer, and thus end the nightly lessons.[35]

Papago

Dream teaching was also an important part of Papago education. The information was usually presented in the form of a song, which was never revealed to others.[36] Dream songs were powerful forces; they were awe-inspiring and sacred. With these dream songs, the Papago brought life-giving rain, ensured the growth of crops, healed the sick and performed numerous other positive actions.[37]

Male shamans within ancient Papago societies obtained their power through dream songs. They often began hearing these at an early age, and such songs usually continued through adulthood. Eventually, a man who had heard many songs would announce that he would become a shaman.[38] Many such dream songs were revealed by animals who spoke in human voices.[39]

One Papago man, in a state of great depression, went to a cave in a butte near what is now Tempe, Arizona, either to die or to, perhaps, initiate the process of becoming a shaman. He smoked a "magic" reed that he found in the cave and immediately fell asleep. He dreamed that a spirit in human form unknown to him appeared, offering to teach him the art of healing.[40]

The spirit tied a cobweb around that butte and then stretched it to Tempe Butte, from there to Four Peaks, hence to the San Francisco Mountains, and finally to Needles. The spirit guided the dreamer along the cobweb, revealing many cures to him at each mountain. Though he was warned to keep this information confidential, the dreamer later spoke of the knowledge that he had received. In a new dream, the spirit told him that he had learned only half of his lessons, but since he had revealed his lessons to others, he would learn no more. The spirit said that he had learned enough to be an effective healer. This man, who became famous for curing bowel complaints, was frequently chided in later life for having revealed the spirit's lessons.[41]

OTHER NATIVE AMERICAN PEOPLES

Puberty rites involving vision quests (the production of visions or dreams during ritual periods) were in use among many Native American groups. Among the Menomini, such vision quests were performed by both girls and boys. If, after the ritual preparations, a young girl who has just experienced menarche saw in her dream the moon, the sun, stars, an eagle, a thunderbird, or other lofty things, she would enjoy a long, happy life and perhaps an elevation in social status. Dreams also appeared to girls in which spirits revealed their future magical or spiritual abilities.[42]

Among the Zuni, naturally received dreams were sources of inspiration and information. After sleep, women potters often discovered that, in their dreams, they had been given a totally new design to paint onto their pots.[43]

The Cherokee laid such importance on dreams that dreaming of being bitten by a rattlesnake demanded immediate action. The dreamer was treated in the same manner as a person who had actually received a snakebite during waking hours.[44]

The Paiute regarded dreams, not as harbingers of illness, but as the direct cause of sickness itself. A dream-induced sickness might not affect the dreamer; a close relative could fall victim to the disease. Dreams in which the dreamer saw herself or himself as being sick, that include the approach of a shaman, or in which the dreamer hears a voice, were all causes of illness.[45]

This short summary of the significance of dreams among a few Native American tribes is representative of the nearly universal significance given to dreams by the original inhabitants of North America.

Chapter 8

DREAM BOOKS

The earliest extant dream book was written in Egypt in about 2000 B.C.E., although it remains in incomplete form. Fragments of tablets containing dreams and their interpretations were found in the library of Ashurbanipal at Nineveh, but these, too, are incomplete.

As previously stated, the only surviving comprehensive work of dream interpretation from the ancient world is Artemidorus' *The Interpretation of Dreams (Oneirocritica)*, circa 140 C.E.

The five volumes of this work summarized everything then known about dream interpretation (see Chapter 5).

The *Oneirocritica* enjoyed great popularity. The first printed edition of the book appeared in Venice in 1518.[1] Later editions were produced in Basel in 1539 and in Lyons in 1546. The first English translation appeared in London in 1644 and by 1740 it had been through its 24th printing.[2] Artemidorus' work continues to form the basis of dream books to the current day.

Following the success of the *Oneirocritica*, publishers began issuing a number of other dream books. In England these were usually cheaply produced rehashes of Artemidorus' masterwork. The invention of moveable type, and the survival of the *Oneirocritica*, laid the foundation for popularized dream dictionaries.

Chapbooks and pamphlets promising to reveal the meanings of dreams were widely published in England during the eighteenth and nineteenth centuries. They often bore such lurid titles as *The Old Egyptian Fortune-Teller's Last Legacy*, *The Royal Dream Book*, and *The Three Witches*. Most were no longer than twenty-four pages.[3]

In 1767, the first American guide to dream interpretation was published in Boston: *The New Book of Knowledge*. It contained both dream symbols and astrological information. A lengthier volume, *The Universal Interpreter of Dreams and Visions*, appeared in Baltimore in 1795. This work included a dream dictionary largely compiled from Artemidorus.[4]

These early publishers soon had many imitators. By the late 1800s, American mail order companies and traveling salespersons sold inexpensive dream books by the thousands to rural residents. Many homes possessed only two volumes: the Bible and a dream book.

An examination of dream books published in the last 200 years reveals that their compilers made few changes in the dream interpretations that had been accepted since antiquity. Archaic (or nonfashionable) symbols were removed, interpretations were modernized, and a few new symbols (gas lamps, trains, electric lights, subways, cars, and rockets) were added as these inventions came into common use.[5]

The interpretations contained in these books were often quite straightforward: dreaming of gold signified riches; swimming in stormy waters, future troubles; flowers, good luck; books, a change in business.

The ancient concept that dreams can't always be taken literally survived in these works. A dream's "true" meaning may be the reverse of the most obvious interpretation. Thus, dreaming of sickness means eventual recovery; pain presages a happy future event; birth, a loss; stabbing, good fortune. Sexual dreams have completely nonsexual meanings; nonerotic dreams may have sexual components, all of which psychoanalysts term "dream displacement,"[6] while dream books often sum up this phenomenon as "dreams go by contraries."[7] As we've seen, this concept is at least 4,000 years old.

Nineteenth-century dream books weren't limited to interpretations. Poems, lists of lucky days, and essays on subjects from gambling to marriage were also included. Information concerning card reading, palmistry and other minor divinitory arts also found their way into these works.

Dozens of similar dream books are now on the market and can be found in book stores across the United States. Most of these bear remarkable resemblances to those published 100 years ago, following the same alphabetical listing of dreams and their meanings and including most of the familiar symbols.

Such books ignore Artemidorus' advice to interpret the dream in relation to the dreamer's individuality. Most of their authors make no mention of the dreamer's unique qualities (gender, age, profession, relationship status, health, cultural background, religion, ideology), all of which can greatly alter a dream's interpretation.

Because we are individuals, we have individual world views and symbolic languages. Symbols affect us in dramatically idiosyncratic ways. Though there are a few universal human symbols, the majority of dream symbols have profoundly different meanings to each individual.

One old dream book boldly states: "To see a lion, hope for better days." No rationale is given for this statement; it is expected that the reader will trust the author's words.

This interpretation leaves much to be desired. A person who, as a child, was frightened by a lion in a zoo might not see this animal as a positive dream symbol. Conversely, a person who loves lions and cats might accept this interpretation. A worshipper of Isis, Bast, or Sekhmet might give this dream a sacred interpretation, or even recognize it as a visit from the Goddess Herself. Someone allergic to cats could have quite a different interpretation, as might someone who has recently lost a beloved feline companion.

Water is a common dream symbol. Dream books traditionally interpret the sighting of water to indicate a future loving relationship or friendship. However, if the person has a distinct memory of nearly drowning, or if the water takes the form of a stormy sea, a far different personal interpretation is possible.

Dream interpretation is far too complex to be adequately accomplished by referring to dream catalogues. Since dreams emerge from within ourselves (or, in the case of divine dreams, from our deities), only the dreamer can truly pick them apart and discover their hidden meanings (see Chapter 14). Why, then have these books enjoyed great popularity for so many centuries? Humans have always searched for relatively simple methods of peering into the future. Hundreds of forms of divination have been practiced, including dream interpretation using standardized dream books. The fact that these works are the least reliable method of interpreting these messages hasn't lessened their popularity.

Fortunately, as the scientific investigation of dreams has begun, and interest in them has soared, a new breed of dream books has appeared. Some of these analyze the process of dreaming itself. Among these titles are Christopher Evans' *Landscapes of the Night: How and Why We Dream* (New York: Viking Press, 1983); Robert Lang's *Decoding Your Dreams* (New York: Ballantine, 1988); and Peter O'Connor's *Dreams and the Search for Their Meaning* (New York: Paulist Press, 1986).

Other books present new methods of working with dreams to create positive inner changes and healing. These include Stephen LaBerge's *Lucid Dreaming* (New York: Ballantine, 1986) and several works by Patricia Garfield, including *Creative Dreaming* (New York: Ballantine, 1974), *Women's Bodies, Women's Dreams* (New York: Ballantine, 1988) and *The Healing Power of Dreams* (New York: Simon and Schuster, 1991).

Standardized dream books will continue to be published in the future. Many persons will eagerly turn to them each morning, searching for clues of the day's events.

Fortunately, the new dream books are bringing order and logic to this process, and thus are providing dreamers with valuable tools, not only for dream interpretation, but for the enhancement of spirituality and the improvement of our individual existences.

II
NIGHT

Chapter 9

Sacred Sleep

The intimate connection between sleep and spirituality has been examined in the last section of this book. These (at times) lengthy excursions into past cultures have been necessary to support my thesis (that dreams can be a method of contacting deity) as well as to lay the foundations for this practice.

From the techniques that enjoyed such popularity in the ancient world, combined with current dream research, we can create a new system of sacred sleep. Some of the procedures have been modified: it isn't necessary to visit a temple to receive a divine dream, and our sacrifices are now of a different character. However, much of the information contained in Part II of this book is directly based on the practices of both old world and new world peoples, combined with the results of personal experience.

SACRED SLEEP DEFINED

By way of explicit definition, sacred sleep is that which occurs following a ritual request for a divinely inspired dream. The term includes ritual preparations, pre-sleep rituals, sleep itself, the recording of dreams, and their interpretation. Sacred sleep is a specific ritual act. Though we can experience divine dreams at any time, only those created as a result of this process are considered to be the products of sacred sleep.

CONCERNS

Before proceeding any further, it is necessary to address a number of questions that some of you are no doubt asking.

Are you suggesting that spiritual beings can be coerced into appearing in our dreams? No. I'm simply stating that we can ask (even plead) that our personal deities present us with needed guidance, inspiration, comfort, or prophetic information within our dreams. All worshippers certainly have the right to request such divine assistance.

Will all goddesses (and/or gods) appear in dreams, or only those historically known for this? History teaches us that some deities were particularly prone to dream visitation, but most ancient cultures accepted that all goddesses and gods could present dreams to their worshippers. This is built on the concept that, during sleep, our subconscious minds (or "souls") are freed from the distractions of everyday life and, thus, are open to receive divine messages. Deities may send such messages at any time, day or night. However, those received in the night are far more likely to be remembered (as dreams) than are those unexpected divine revelations that occur while we try to back into a six-foot parking space. Thus, sleep provides us with an excellent opportunity to strengthen our spiritual contacts.

I'm still not sure that this is right. If this is a concern, realize that sacred sleep was invented by the goddesses and gods themselves—not by humans. If you're questioning the advisability of consciously introducing sleep to your spiritual activities, wait. You may have a dream that answers your concerns.

Why would the Goddess try to contact me? Why not? Spirituality, like nature, abhors a vacuum. A personal relationship with deity is a two-way street. We speak; She or He listens. She or He speaks; we listen. This communication (in the form of prayer, ritual, and meditation) is an integral part of all fulfilling spiritual practices, and can be extended to sleep.

I don't worship a goddess or a god. I attune with my totem animal (or spirit helper, or guide). Can I practice sacred sleep to communicate with Bear? Of course. The form of the spiritual being is not as important as the relationship that you've established with this being.

I'm spiritually adrift. I'm not in contact with any one particular deity. Can I still use sacred sleep? Yes. In fact, dreams can be used to determine the nature of your personal spiritual path. Many Native American cultures used dream quests to discover men's and women's personal spirits (deities) who lent them knowledge, wisdom, and spiritual power. The integration of sacred sleep into your existing spiritual activities is certainly the ideal. When this is impossible, the techniques outlined in this section can be used with slight alterations. You may invoke a likely deity before bed and wait for a reply. Alternately, a general invocation to the Goddess or the God can be used.

Isn't this slightly dangerous? Couldn't we call up evil demons or some other beings that could play with our minds? No, for two reasons. First, what were perceived as evil demons in ancient cultures were largely negative human emotions, specific physical conditions (such as epilepsy), disease, and mental and behavioral disorders. Today, many occultists interpret the concept of demons as misunderstandings of the accumulation of negative energy (lacking consciousness or personality) that naturally occur in areas inhabited by large groups of humans. Demons as devouring, maniacal beings simply don't exist. They can't enter our dreams. Second, the ritual preparations and invocations that precede sacred sleep firmly connect you with your deity. "Demons" simply won't bother you.

How often should I have sacred sleep? Only in time of need. Such needs may include spiritual comfort and reassurance; advice about relationships, families, emotions, relocations, and employment;

glimpses into the future; physical conditions and cycles; concern for animal companions; heart-breaking losses; and other matters.

How will I know if a dream has been divinely inspired, if the Goddess (or God) doesn't actually appear within it? This is an excellent question. Some methods of making this determination are discussed in Chapter 15.

How much weight should I give to divine dreams? This must be a personal decision. If you value your relationship with your personal deity, you'll reflect on such messages and act upon them without delay. Failure to do so may bring another dream of the same type, bearing the same advice. If you ignore three or more identical messages, you should probably suspend sacred sleep, as you are obviously not ready for the advice.

Should I practice sacred sleep during pregnancy? Menstruation? These subjects are cursorily investigated in the next chapter. References to other sources of information concerning these subjects can be found in the notes following Chapter 11.

I hope that I have answered most of your questions. For others that I haven't addressed, dream and let your deity provide the answers.

SACRED SLEEP AS
PERSONAL RELIGION

Sacred sleep is one of the oldest forms of personal spirituality. It recalls a time when religion was not a monotheistic, monolithic, patriarchal business. In earlier days, the veil that separated our world from the realm of the goddesses and gods was thin. Our society has created an iron curtain of doubt and spiritual fear between the two spheres. Only the narrowest forms of religious belief and practice are condoned, and we're expected to place our spiritual practices in the hands of others.

Yet, the surging rebirth of Pagan spirituality (particularly the overwhelming popularity of Goddess worship), and the general broadening of human consciousness, are positive signs that more fulfilling religious structures and practices will continue to take their place in human society far into the future. The age of personal religion has once again arrived.

Sacred sleep is one manifestation of the process of removing spirituality from the hands of the experts and placing it where it belongs: in the hearts, minds, and dreams of the worshippers themselves.

Chapter 10

DREAM MESSENGERS

Part II of this book has been written for those who have established a personal relationship with deity (or with deities). It is this relationship that acts as a conduit of divine wisdom through our dreams.

In sacred sleep, we term as Messengers the deities Who provide us with dreams. These are the deities that we worship in our waking lives, with a slight difference: though we may experience spiritual union with our goddess and/or god at any time during the day, they appear as Messengers only at night in our sleep.

The first section of this book outlined ritual dreaming practices in the ancient world. In contrast to later Western and Middle Eastern religions, earlier peoples had far closer relationships with their conceptions of the divine. Save for the queens and kings of the pantheons, the deities were not distant and cold. They easily and willingly communicated with their worshippers.

Though dreams can be spontaneously received from "foreign" deities (that is, from those with whom we have not attuned), such instances are rare and may be missed by the dreamer due to a lack of familiarity with the deity's symbols and attributes. The clearest messages arrive directly from the deity (or deities) with which we are most familiar.

WESTERN PAGANISM TODAY

The Pagan deities still live. They continue to be concerned with natural phenomena, with early delights, with our problems. They did not die; only the major forms of Their worship were destroyed.

A large number of intelligent Westerners have thrown off the spiritual shackles of monotheistic religion that have bound our hands for 2,000 years. Old religious ideals and conceptions of the divine are being reexamined. Women and men are contacting goddesses and gods from past ages, gleaning ancient truths that have long been suppressed.

Some modern Pagans worship an entire pantheon of goddesses and gods, though many women limit their worship to goddesses alone. (See Margot Adler's *Drawing Down the Moon*.) This is true of both personal worship and of the new forms of ancient religions, including Wicca. Goddess worship in particular, shows strong signs of continuing growth among both men and women. The rebirth of Pagan spirituality is upon us.

It is these Pagan deities that are most likely to appear in sacred sleep, and this book is slanted in Their favor. I make no apologies for this bias. For two millennia, goddesses and gods touched the lives of their worshippers with healing, prophetic, and comforting dreams. The gifts received in the ancient sleep temples have never been equalled.

If you have established a relationship with a deity, you are probably familiar with Her or His sacred stories (myths), attributes, and symbols. However, the listings that follow of principal attributes, symbols, and appearances (where known) are included here to ensure that you will recognize the symbols of your deity when She or He arrives in your dream.

If You Haven't Found Your Messenger

If, by some chance, you haven't yet attuned with a deity, the information contained in Part III of this book (recalling, recording, and interpreting dreams) is still of value and can be used by all persons for dream interpretation.

Additionally, in moments of crisis, a dream ritual can certainly be used, even by those who have no connections with divinities (see Chapter 11). If a goddess or god does unexpectedly appear in a dream, see it as a sign that she or he is willing to listen and assist with your problems.

The Lists

The first list in the next section includes Egyptian, Sumerian, Babylonian, Assyrian, Greek, and Roman deities. Though Celtic deities lie outside the scope of this work, I've appended a second list describing their attributes, due to the continuing resurgence of interest in Celtic goddesses and gods.

These lists are far from all-inclusive. Research into sacred stories ("mythology") will present the interested reader with a wealth of further information. Additionally, Appendix 1 consists of a list of divine dream symbols and their attendant deities, and Appendix 2 is an alphabetical listing of dream and sleep deities.

DEITIES, APPEARANCES, AND SYMBOLS

Adad: (Babylonian) God of storms, rain, and omens. Symbols: bull, lightning, pickaxe, cypress, mountain, riches, the number 6.

Aesculapius: (Greek, Roman) God of healing. May appear as a handsome, bearded man, seated on a throne and holding a staff wrapped with a living snake, or even as a snake or dog. Symbols: snake, caduceus (a staff entwined with a snake), dog.

Amon: (Egyptian) God of the wind. Symbols: Goose, ram.

Amor: (Roman) God of love. May appear as a winged youth. Symbols: torch, bow, arrow.

Anu: (Sumerian) Father of the deities. Symbols: horned altar, bull, diadem, scepter, tamarisk (tree), stars, the number 60.

Anubis: (Egyptian) God of the dead who presides over funerals and guided souls. May appear as a jackal-headed man. Symbols: jackal, scales.

Aphrodite: (Greek) Goddess of love, beauty and war. May appear naked, partially clothed, or fully clothed, perhaps in a tunic. May also be seen rising from the sea or driving a chariot. Symbols: shield, arrow, helmet, sword, rose, myrtle, apple, poppy, sparrow, dove, swallow, competitions, fish, garden, swan, the planet Venus, the month of April.

Apis: (Egyptian) Greek name for Hapi, the sacred bull of Memphis. Originally a fertility deity. Symbol: bull.

Apollo: (Greek) God of music, arts, theater, healing, prophecy and archery. May appear as a nude young man. Symbols: lyre, raven, swan, bay (laurel).

Artemis: (Greek) Virgin Goddess of the Hunt. Rules and protects wild animals and childbirth. May appear as a huntress wandering the forests, or driving a chariot drawn by two white stags, and holding Her bow and quiver. Symbols: birth, deer, lion, dog, arrow, bow, quiver, hair, rooster, moon, bay (laurel).

Ashnan: (Babylonian) Goddess of wheat. Symbols: grain, plow.

Asklepios: See Aesculapius.

Athena: (Greek) Tutelary deity of Athens, originally Cretan. Unmarried (i.e., "virgin") goddess of wisdom, war, and peace. Symbols: armor, helmet, shield, rake, bridle, snake, owl, olive.

Bacchus: (Roman) God of fertility and wine. Symbols: wine, vine, grapes, pine cone.

Bast: (Egyptian) Goddess of music, dance, joy, happiness, perfume, and spiritual love. Often seen as a woman with a cat's head, holding a sistrum, with kittens at Her feet. May also appear as a cat. Symbols: cat, lion, sistrum. An alternate name is Bastet.

Bes: (Egyptian) God of protection (especially of children), childbirth, prosperity, and dance. He also encouraged human carnal activity. Bes was invoked in ancient Egypt before sleep

for protection and to send favorable dreams.
Usually appears as a squat, dwarfish figure
with bent legs, either nude or wearing a lion
skin. Symbols: musical instruments such as
the tambourine (the sound of which warded
off evil), knife.

Ceres: (Roman) Goddess of agriculture, fertility,
and marriage. Symbols: grain, fruit, flowers,
bread.

Demeter: (Greek) Goddess of the Earth and
fertility. May reveal Herself as either walking
or seated, always fully attired; at times, She
appears in a chariot. Symbols: grain, pine
cone, pig, food (in general), cave, barley, beer,
bee, bread, snake.

Diana: (Roman) Goddess of virginity, the moon,
the woods, hunting. May appear as a
huntress. Symbols: crescent moon, the moon
itself, bow, dog, trees.

Dionysius: (Greek) God of fertility, wine and
drunkenness. May be seen as a goat, a bull or
a drunken man. Symbols: vine, grape, pine
cone, ivy, fig, ship.

Dumuzi: (Sumerian) God of vegetation and the
male force in nature.

Ea: (Babylonian) God of wisdom, sweet waters, magic, arts and storms. Symbols: water, goat-fish, copper, ram, the star Dilgan, the constellation Aquarius, the number 40.

Enlil: (Sumerian) God of the wind; supreme god of Sumer. Symbols: pickaxe, headdress decorated with horns, mountain, the stars (generally), the constellation Pleiades.

Eos: (Greek) Goddess of the dawn. Symbols: dew, chariot.

Eris: (Greek) Goddess of discord and of competitions. Symbols: apple, competitions.

Eros: (Greek) God of love. May appear as a naked, winged young man armed with a bow and gold-tipped arrows. Symbols: bow, arrows.

Fauna: (Roman) Goddess of oracular dreams, the earth, health, and domesticated animals.

Faunus: (Roman) God of nature and protector of shepherds. Sender of dreams. May be seen horned. Symbols: cow, trees.

Flora: (Roman) Goddess of flowers, grain, and human sexuality. Symbols: flowers, spring.

Fortuna: (Roman) Goddess of women and good fortune. Symbols: rudder, cornucopia, globe, wheel of fortune, riches.

Gaea: (Greek) Goddess of the Earth, marriage, and prophecy. Symbols: cornucopia, vapors, key, fruits and vegetables. (A popular modern symbol of Gaea is a photograph of the Earth taken from outer space.)

Gatumdug: (Babylonian/Assyrian) Goddess of milk. Symbol: milk.

Geb: (Egyptian) God of the Earth. May appear as a human male wearing the crown of Lower Egypt (or a goose) on His head. Symbols: the crown of Lower Egypt, goose.

Geshtinanna: (Babylonian/Assyrian) Goddess of brewing, "divine interpretress of dreams." Symbols: vine, wine, beer.

Gula: (Sumerian) Goddess of healing. Symbol: dog.

Hamarkis: (Egyptian) An aspect of Horus identified with the Sphinx long after its creation. Symbol: sphinx.

Hapi: (Egyptian) God of the Nile. May appear as a well-fed man or a monkey.

Harakty: See Ra-Harakty.

Hathor: (Egyptian) Goddess of the sky, dancing, music and love; mother goddess; "Lady of the House of Jubilation." May appear as a cow, as a cow-headed woman, or as a woman with cow horns on Her head. Symbols: milk, sistrum, cow, date palm, sycamore, trees (generally).

Hecate: (Greek) Originally, a goddess of the moon, the earth, and the sea; Her blessings were wealth, victory, wisdom, and successful hunting. Later in Greek history, a goddess of darker magics and sorcery. May appear as an ordinary woman, or as a three-faced woman followed by howling dogs. Symbols: crossroads, snakes, torch, dog, the moon.

Heket: (Egyptian) Goddess of love, fertility, and childbirth. May be seen as a frog. Symbols: frog, birth.

Helios: (Greek) God of the sun; He Who "sees and hears all." Was invoked to witness solemn oaths. May be seen in a chariot drawn by horses; sometimes as winged.

Hephaestus: (Greek) God of fire, smithing and crafts. Symbols: hammer, anvil.

Hera: (Greek) Goddess of marriage and childbirth, queen of all deities. Guardian of the vows of wedlock. Symbols: cow, peacock, diadem, scepter, apple, pomegranate, birth, chariot, veil.

Hermes: (Greek) Messenger of the gods; protector of homes; giver of luck; the divine dream guide. May be seen carrying a ram or holding a lyre, or as a winged young man wearing winged shoes and a hat, holding a staff. Symbols: lyre, piles of stones, treaties, sandals, roads, riches, gymnastics instructors, flute, pillars, ram, hat, competitions.

Hestia: (Greek) Goddess of the hearth and of fire. Symbols: hearth, fireplace, fire, home.

Horus: (Egyptian) God of the sky and of protection. May be seen as hawkheaded. Symbols: hawk, eye.

Hygeia: (Greek) Goddess of good health. May be seen giving water to snakes from a bowl. Symbols: snake, bowl.

Hypnos: (Greek) God of sleep. May be seen as two of His symbols: a winged young man holding a poppy and a small horn.

Inanna: (Sumerian) Goddess of love, war, the planet Venus. May appear naked, with rays of light surrounding Her, or as a huntress.

Symbols: a reed bundle, bow, dog, lion, the moon, the planet Venus.

Iris: (Greek) The herald of the deities. She may be seen as a winged being, holding a herald's staff, and traveling on a rainbow. Symbols: herald's staff, rainbow.

Ishtar: (Babylonian/Assyrian) Goddess of sex, love, war, and hunting. Queen of heaven. Symbols: bow, snake, quiver, dog, dove, lion, moon, star, eight-pointed star, sixteen-pointed star, rosette, the number 15, the planet Venus.

Isis: (Egyptian) Goddess of love, magic, healing, childbirth, the earth, the moon, protector of the dead, restorer of the dead, sailing, cultivated land, fields, agriculture, food, water, lighthouses, justice, beer, riches, weaving, education, nursing, mourning, the underworld—to name a few of Her attributes. May be seen as a woman wearing a headdress in the shape of a vulture, holding a papyrus scepter and an ankh, standing or enthroned; wearing a headdress consisting of a disc surrounded by horns (sun and moon); as a mother suckling her son (Horus). Symbols: thet (buckle), throne, sistrum, ankh, kite (bird), shuttle, uraeus, bread, rudder, linen garments, riches, lotus (water lily), milk, moon, torch, the stars Sirius (Sothis) and Antares.

Janus: (Roman) God of doors, gateways and law. May appear as a male possessing two faces. Symbol: door.

Juno: (Roman) Goddess of marriage and birth; protectress of married women. Symbols: peacock, door, goat, birth.

Jupiter: (Roman) God of the sky, light, rain, lightning, and war. Symbols: pebble, oak, mountain, white cap, chariot, flint, scepter.

Ki: (Sumerian) Ancient creation goddess. Later identified with Ninhursag.

Lathar: (Sumerian) God of the cattle. Symbol: cow.

Liber: (Roman) God of wine and of fertility. His feast took place on March 17. Symbols: wine, vine, grape.

Luna: (Greek) Goddess of the moon; Luna is an epithet of Artemis. Symbol: moon.

Marduk: (Sumerian) God of exorcism, healing, wisdom, and judgment; bringer of light; the head of the Sumerian pantheon. Symbols: musussu (dragon-like creature), shovel, pickaxe, sickle, clay writing tablet, lead (metal), and the planet Jupiter.

Mars: (Roman) God of war and protector of the fields. Symbols: lance, shield, woodpecker, wolf and bull.

Mercury: (Roman) God of business, industry, riches and profit.

Min: (Egyptian) God of fertility. Usually appears as a man with an erection. Symbols: lettuce, phallus.

Minerva: (Roman) Goddess of wisdom, protector of crafts workers, artisans, and teachers. Symbols: owl, olive, helmet, the number 5.

Nabu: (Babylonian/Assyrian) Scribe of the deities. God of writing. Symbols: stylus, shovel, clay tablet.

Nanna: (Sumerian) God of the moon and of justice; "lord of destiny." Symbol: the moon, crescent.

Nanshe: (Sumerian) Goddess of dreams, ethics and morals. The "divine interpretress of dreams."

Nekhbet: (Egyptian) Tutelary goddess of the pharaoh and goddess of childbirth. Symbols: vulture, rod of authority.

Ningirsu: (Sumerian) God of fertility, fields, and war. Symbols: lion-headed eagle (named Imdugud), the number 50.

Ninhursag: (Sumerian) Primeval goddess of mountains. Mother of all living things. Also known as Ninmah ("exalted lady"), Nintu ("the lady who gives birth"), Mami and Ninmu. Symbols: plants (generally).

Ninkasi: (Sumerian) Goddess of beer and bread; divine brewer of the deities. Symbols: beer, bread.

Ninsun: (Sumerian) Goddess of wisdom and interpreter of dreams. Mother of Gilgamesh.

Ninurta: (Sumerian) God of war, the fields, fertility, and the stormy North wind. Symbols: dog, gypsum, reeds.

Nisaba: (Sumerian) Goddess of writing, knowledge, understanding, and grain. "She Who opens the ears." Symbols: grain, stylus, barley.

Nut: (Egyptian) Sky goddess; goddess of resurrection. May be seen as a naked female figure stretched across the sky, as a "sky cow," or as a bee. Symbols: a starry blue cloak, the color blue, pig.

Osiris: (Egyptian) God of fertility, agriculture, dance, death and resurrection. May be seen as a mummy (wrapped only up to the neck), with a beard and wearing a white crown. Symbols: crook, flail, hare.

Pan: (Greek) God of fields and woods. May be seen as a very hairy human male with goat's hooves, horns, and a beard. Symbols: pan pipes, flute, forest, goat, hunting, trees.

Persephone: (Greek) Goddess of vegetation, fertility, and the underworld (for four months each year). Symbols: grain, pomegranate, plants (generally), scepter.

Pomona: (Roman) Goddess of ripening fruit. Symbols: fruit, apple.

Poseidon: (Greek) God of the sea. May be seen as a horse dashing on the beach, or in the waves. Symbols: horse, trident, lightning, earthquakes, dolphin, horse races, sailing, chariot.

Ptah: (Egyptian) Creator god; god of crafts. May appear as a man wrapped (like a mummy) to the neck.

Ra: (Egyptian) God of the sun. Symbols: obelisks, falcon, ship.

Ra-Harakty: (Egyptian) God of the morning sun. Symbols: falcon.

Salus: (Roman) Goddess of health; protectress against illness. Symbols: snake, bowl.

Sekhmet: (Egyptian) Goddess of war, healing, magic, lust and passion. May appear as lioness or a lion-headed woman. Symbols: hot winds, desert, cat, lion, scorpion.

Selket: (Egyptian) Goddess of magic and protection. Sometimes seen as a female with a scorpion on Her head; at other times, as possessing a scorpion body with a human head. Symbol: scorpion.

Serapis: (Ptolemaic form of Osiris-Apis) God of healing in ancient Greece, Rome, and Egypt. May appear as a bull. Symbol: bull.

Set: (Egyptian) God of adversity and the personification of evil. Symbols: antelope, crocodile.

Shala: (Assyrian) Goddess of grain. Symbol: grain.

Shamash: (Babylonian) God of justice and the sun. Symbols: lion, saw, the number 20.

Sin: (Babylonian/Assyrian) God of the moon, lord of destiny. Symbols: crescent, bull, dragon, boat, the sickle moon, calendar, the number 30.

Spes: (Roman) Goddess of hope. May appear as a young woman bearing flowers or grain. Symbols: grain, gardens.

Thoth: (Egyptian) God of the moon, writing, and the calendar. May be seen as having an ibis' head. Symbols: ibis, palm, calendar.

Tyche: (Greek) Goddess of fortune and fate. Symbols: cornucopia, wheel, globe, ball, rudder.

Utu: (Babylonian/Assyrian) God of the sun and of justice.

Uttu: (Sumerian) Goddess of plants, weaving and clothing.

Vesta: (Roman) Goddess of the hearth and of fire. No images were made of Her. Symbols: hearth, fireplace, fire, home, donkey.

Vulcan: (Roman) God of smithing and of fire; also guarded against fires. Symbols: anvil, fire, hammer.

Zeus: (Greek) Supreme god; god of weather, rain, lightning, snow, judgment, and freedom. Symbols: oak, dew, cuckoo bird, bee, bull, swan, eagle, justice, white poplar, snake.

Celtic Deities

Angus Mac Og: (Irish) A god of love. Usually seen as a youth.

Anu: (Irish) Mother Goddess; provider of plenty.

Badb: (Irish) Goddess of war. Symbol: the crow.

Bress: (Irish) God of fertility and agriculture.

Brigit: (Irish) Goddess of healing, smithcraft, poetry, and inspiration; associated with purificatory fires. Actually a three-fold goddess. She seems to have been worshipped solely by women.

Cerridwen: (Welsh) Goddess of the moon and of grain; provider of wisdom. She possesses a cauldron of regeneration and inspiration. Widely worshipped by contemporary Wiccans and Pagans. Symbol: cauldron.

Cernunnos: (Celtic) Horned god; possibly a deity of fertility and wealth, or of the underworld. Usually seen sitting cross-legged, bearing antlers on His head. Worshipped by many contemporary Pagans and Wiccans.

Dagda, the: (Irish) "The Good God"; giver of fertility and abundance; overseer of contracts. Symbols: a massive club; a cauldron of food that is never exhausted; a magic harp on which songs of sleep, woe, and laughter can be played.

Danu: (Irish) Mother Goddess.

Diancecht: (Irish) God of medicine with the power to miraculously heal all wounds.

Dylan: (Welsh) God of the sea.

Epona: (British and Gaulish) Goddess of the horse; Mother Goddess. During the Roman period, cavalry units worshipped Her. Usually seen riding a white horse. Symbols: horse, cornucopia, dog.

Goibniu: (Irish) God of divine weapon-forging. Divine brewer.

Govannon: (Welsh) God of smithcraft.

Herne: (British) Horned god of the wild hunt.

Lugh: (Irish) God of magic, war, poetry, art, and handicrafts. Symbols: raven, spear.

Mabon: (Welsh) God of hunting.

Manannan Mac Lir: (Irish, Manx) God of the sea, ruler of the "Land of the Blessed" (the joyous realm of the deceased). Forecasted the weather for sailors. Often seen riding the waves in a chariot. Symbol: cauldron.

Morrigan: (Irish) Goddess of war. Appeared as a raven before and during battles. Symbol: crow or raven.

Ogma: (Irish) God of wisdom and writing. He developed the earliest Irish Dream Messengers' alphabet, the Ogham script, in about 400 C.E.

Rhiannon: (Welsh) Goddess of fertility, the underworld, and possibly the moon. Symbol: white horse.

Sirona: (Welsh) Goddess of springs and wells, and possibly of the stars.

Tailtiu: (Irish) Goddess of the earth and of natural forces.

Chapter 11

PREPARATIONS FOR SACRED SLEEP

Since sacred sleep is an act of union with our deities, it is wise to ensure that we're in a clear, calm, and focused spiritual state before retiring. Asking a goddess or god for a dream message while drunkenly falling into bed almost guarantees a lack of results.

The suggestions that follow are just that—suggestions. Your actual preparations for sacred sleep may vary for a number of reasons: your environment (no bathtub; an ocean nearby);

your health (not eating after dark may imperil your life during certain illnesses); the nature of your Messenger (don't eat fish just before invoking a goddess that forbids the eating of fish); and other factors.

The following discussions are based on ancient practices as well as personal experience. Feel free to use them in preparing for sacred sleep.

TIMING

Timing can be of great importance in determining when to practice sacred sleep. A feast day associated with your goddess or god would be highly appropriate, as would seasons or months directly or indirectly connected with the deity (spring for plant goddesses and gods; summer for sexual deities; fall for harvest deities; winter for darker deities). This may mean quite a wait.

The Moon

A second method involves the phases of the moon. The moon has a significant effect on the human body, mind, and emotions, and its phases can be a useful guide:

Waxing Moon: Questions involving new ventures, creativity, fertility, growth, healing, love, joyous emotions, relationships, health, conception, childbirth, babies in general, money, families.

Full Moon: Questions of all types (including those listed above and below).

Waning Moon: Questions regarding the past, past lives, wisdom, sources of knowledge, teachers, depressing emotions, endings.

Lunar goddesses are, of course, best invoked at the phase that most closely matches Their influences.

Cycles

Human cycles are yet another factor that can be used to determine the ideal night for sacred sleep. Many women acknowledge that menstruation marks a time of greatly enhanced spiritual power. The male fear of women's power during menstruation, evident in many cultures, may have been the unacknowledged reason for the male concept that women are "unclean."

Because menstruation is a time of increased power, many women discover that their dreams are radically altered. Dreams at such times may be far more active and involved with sex, violence, and conversations with animals, among other experiences.[1] In addition, though the true nature of PMS is currently under discussion, it is possible that longer periods of sleep each day late in a woman's cycle can offer her the means to dream away many of the undesirable effects of this often-trying time.[2] Since sacred sleep just before and during menstruation produces more vivid and powerful dreams,[3] this may well be an excellent time to ask a deity (specifically a goddess) for a sacred dream.

During pregnancy, most women experience an increased number of dreams.[4] This may be due to the deeper levels of sleep that women experience during the early stages of pregnancy.[5]

Sacred sleep can be practiced during pregnancy, but it will probably be most productive in the first and second trimesters. By the third trimester, the dramatic physiological changes occurring within the woman's body often disturb sleep. Dreams near the end of pregnancy tend to be concerned solely with the baby and with the pregnancy itself.[6] However, during all stages of pregnancy, asking for dreams from goddesses associated with childbirth seems quite reasonable.

The Next Day

Another consideration is far more mundane: will you be able to awaken naturally on the following morning? Ancient texts confirm that most divinely inspired dreams occur in the last few hours of sleep, when the soul is freest from mundane influences.[7] Having an alarm clock (or a child) jolting you from sacred sleep is far from the ideal, and may well prevent you from completing an important dream. If this is a problem, plan sacred sleep when you won't have to rise with an alarm clock the following morning.

Finally, having laid out this feast of choices, I'm forced to state that none of them are truly necessary. Sacred sleep can and should be used when needed. It can certainly be utilized as an emergency measure at any time.

Trust yourself. You'll know when to call your messenger.

DIET

Eat lightly before dusk prior to sacred sleep; eat little or nothing after sundown. Heavy meals and meats should be avoided if at all possible. These tend to distract the psychic mind, and thus prevent the appropriate connection with deity. Artemidorus states that the dreams caused by "immoderate" eating before sleep shouldn't be examined, for overindulgence prevents truthful dreams.[8]

Easily digested foods (fish and lightly steamed vegetables) are the ideal. Many foods are linked with deities, and these can be eaten during the day as a part of your special dream diet.

Fasting and extreme diets were often a prerequisite to ancient dream incubation,[9] but there is no need to starve yourself before sacred sleep. Medically supervised fasting can have its spiritual uses, but it's not necessary for our purposes.

ALCOHOL AND PRESCRIPTION DRUGS

Galen wrote that wine was forbidden for up to fifteen days prior to sacred sleep.[10] Philostros wrote that wine was banned from the temple of Asklepios at Pergamon because it soiled the "ether of the soul."[11] He also wrote that dream interpreters refused to hear dreams that had occurred under the influence of alcohol.[12] Most other ancient cultures agreed that the dreamer should be free from alcohol for at least twenty-four hours before incubation.

Research performed in the last three decades seems to suggest that certain drugs inhibit the production of dreams, including alcohol,[13] tranquilizers, and sleeping pills,[14] but that caffeine may actually stimulate dreams.[15] The nature of caffeine's role in producing dreams is unclear, but perhaps, after caffeine's stimulating effects have largely worn off, sufficient levels of this alkaloid remain in the system to stimulate the mind during sleep, thus producing dreams. Despite caffeine's potential for enhancing the production of dreams, it isn't recommended as it can inhibit sleep itself.

Alcohol should be considered to be a non-sacred and limiting influence for sacred sleepers. It's best to avoid alcohol, tranquilizers, and sleeping pills before sacred sleep.

CHASTITY

The idea that sex is "unclean" seems to have developed as a male method of imposing social control over women, and is most certainly directly linked with menstruation. Many earlier cultures, however, integrated sex (symbolic or actual) in certain festivals. Additionally, temple prostitution, involving both men and women, was a common practice in

Mesopotamia. A strong sexual element can be found in the religious rites of ancient Egypt, Babylon, Greece, Rome, and Britain; in Africa, China, Japan, India, Micronesia, Melanesia, and Polynesia. Even medieval European churches contain sexually explicit carvings.

Still, most ancient Mediterranean cultures were fairly adamant: sexual relations were not permitted before sacred sleep. The amount of time varied, but it was usually at least twenty-four hours. Temple records continuously state that "the dreamer was pure."

Today, we have different views concerning sex, and few women consider themselves to be "unclean." Sexual activity before sacred sleep need not be of great concern and, indeed, sex before asking a sexual goddess or god for a dream could be highly appropriate. I would suggest, however, performing your dream ritual after sex, not before.

Chapter 12

Dream Rituals

We are unique individuals. Though all humans share common characteristics, our inner selves display great variety. Rituals to produce divine dreams are best tailored to meet our specific personalities. They should reflect ourselves, the nature of the Messenger and our relationship with her or him.

There are many factors to be considered when designing personal dream rituals. Dream rituals for goddesses may well be quite different from those directed toward gods. The culture from which the deity sprang can affect the structure of the dream rite. Depending on the nature of your need, you may plead for assistance or reverently request help. If you're newly establishing a divine relationship, you may also wish to emphasize this fact in your rite. Dream rituals can even be structured so as to simultaneously call two deities.

This chapter outlines one system of creating dream rituals. Each of the steps is discussed, followed by two sample dream rituals.

Creating dream rituals isn't terribly difficult. Free yourself from doubts concerning your creativity. Write something that will move you. If nothing else, utilize the shorter ritual (at the end of this chapter) to contact your personal deity through your dreams.

THE STRUCTURE OF DREAM RITUALS

1. Compose the question

2. Compose the prayer

3. Purify the self

4. Don special garments and jewelry, or nothing

5. Create the altar (if necessary)

6. Purify the bedroom

7. Offerings

8. Invocation

9. Bed

10. Assume a ritual sleep posture (if desired)

11. Sleep

12. Dream

Compose the Question

It is always best to ask your messenger deity a specific question. Queries such as "What's going to happen in the next year?" are far more difficult to answer (since you largely affect this) than are more specific questions, such as "What can I do to find love?" or "Should I leave my job?" Thus, decide your greatest need and focus your question to ensure a direct answer.

Write your question on a piece of paper. Rewrite it several times, cutting words and clarifying its form. When you're satisfied with your question, incorporate it into your prayer as follows.

Compose the Prayer

This prayer is, among other aspects of dream rituals, the key that unlocks the avenue to divine communication. It should therefore be highly personal.

Though you're certainly free to write according to your own vision, here are some guidelines, in the order they could appear in the prayer:

1. Mention the deity by name. (The first word of the prayer may be the name.)

2. Mention the deity's main attribute and title (especially if they're directly linked with your request: "Mistress of Healing," "Giver of Life," "Keeper of Wisdom," and so on.)

3. Name yourself as a worshipper of the deity.

4. Praise the deity. (Glorify her or his power.)

5. Name some of the deity's attributes and symbols. (Moon, animals, tools, etc. See Appendix 1.)

6. Praise the deity.

7. Say something to the effect of "Hear my prayer."

8. Ask that the deity appear in (or affect) your dream that night. There are many romantic

methods of accomplishing this: "Stand by me tonight," and "Travel the road of dreams and reveal yourself," are two examples.

9. Praise the deity.

10. Ask again that the deity appear in your dream.

11. Praise the deity.

12. Ask your dream question.

13. Praise the deity.

14. Thank the deity for her or his attendance. Some representative fragments of dream prayers include the following:

Goddess of the moon, ruler of night. . . .
Reveal Yourself to me and let me see a
favorable dream.
Keeper of all secrets,
Divine bearer of wisdom. . . .
Present me with the information
that I require.
May the Truthful Seer come out of
the holy shrine.
Come out of the night.
Come in this very night.

When you've finished composing your prayer, write out a clean copy of it, without corrections or changes.

Your prayer can be in poetic form, but the rigid structure of this literary genre may actually inhibit the prayer's power, for you'll have to use words that maintain the poem's scan and rhyme, rather than those that are most appropriate.

Then again, you may feel that the method outlined above is also too structured. If so, write according to your inner feelings, but ensure that the following are mentioned in your prayer: the deity name, your request for help (question), and your thanks for the deity's attendance.

You needn't write a new prayer every time you practice sacred sleep (if you call to the same deity each time). Simply place your new question into the prayer.

Purification of Self

The supplicants who visited most ancient sleep temples, who were already free of heavy foods, alcohol, and recent sexual congress, had to undergo further purifications. This often took the form of a bath in cold water, salted water, or even in water drawn from the sea. Indeed, many Roman oracular temples were specifically situated beside springs and other sources of water for this very purpose.

Just before your ritual, take a bath in warm water to which you've added a handful of sea salt. Avoid reading or doing anything while soaking in the tub except concentrating on your Messenger. (If you have no bathtub, take a shower and lightly rub your body with rock salt. Rinse.) It isn't necessary to wash your hair.

Jewelry and Garments

Before ritual, you may wish to don special garments or jewelry associated with your deity. Isis worshippers wore white linen garments during sacred sleep; indeed, the color white was generally considered to enhance the production of dreams. The symbolism of purity in this color is obvious. You may also wish to sleep nude, if this is your normal "dress," and nudity seems be highly appropriate for deities Who usually appear naked.

If you have a specific piece of jewelry symbolic of your Messenger (a ring or pendant), and don't continuously wear it, the donning of such a divine symbol specifically for ritual is highly appropriate.

Create The Altar (If Necessary)

Ancient sleep temples contained altars, statues of the deity, offering tables, and other sacred furniture. An established altar for the worship of your deity (or deities) can certainly be used. If you have no permanent altar, it is best to address your prayer to a deity image of some kind. This image may be a statue, a drawing, a painting, or some other symbol (shell, pine cone, stone) linked with your divinity. Even a picture from a book can be used. If you're artistically creative, create an image of your own design.

A simple dream altar can be created by placing the deity image on a small table. Before it, set a bowl to receive offerings (see below). The altar can be flanked with blue candles (to represent sleep and dreams) in candle holders (these should be extinguished at the close of your ritual, before sleep). Any other personal worship objects (sistrum, bells) may also find a place on your altar. An incense burner can be situated before the image, behind the offering bowl. The best location for your dream altar is in the bedroom itself, though it may be created in another room if privacy is a concern.

We don't, of course, worship images of the goddesses and gods. We respect them as keys to our deities. Though they may represent only the outer form of our goddesses and gods, going before them with ritual intent can create powerful internal changes within our beings. Seeing these images awakens our spiritual selves and prepares us for sacred sleep.

Purification of the Bedroom

In Egypt, and elsewhere, the dream temples were purified with incense. Fragrant barks, resins, and herbs were smoldered on hot coals to purify the temple, to invoke the deity as well as to ritually prepare the dreamers. In Egypt, frankincense and myrrh were most commonly used, as was *kyphi*, an incense described as "delighting in the things of the night."

Frankincense is highly regarded as a tool for purification because it lulls the conscious mind, promotes deep breathing, and generally relaxes those who smell its rich fragrance.

You may prepare your dream chamber for ritual by smoldering a small amount of incense just prior to sleep. Too much incense may, however, interfere with sleep.

Offerings

It is traditional to make an offering during dream rituals. A consumable item of some kind is ideal: wheat bread, fruits, fresh flowers, honey, and even money (which is later donated to the charity or cause of your choice). Place the offering in the bowl (or, in the case of flowers, in a vase) with reverence, while saying appropriate words. (See the first dream ritual below.)

Invocation

Light the candles and incense (if used). Compose yourself. Say your dream prayer. Invocation is the most important aspect of dream rituals. It opens the channels of communication between human and divinity. Though it's best to memorize the prayer, it can be read the first few nights that you use it. State the prayer with emotion and with vocal power. If necessary, whisper, but pack your words with your need.

Bed

The sheets and pillowcases should be freshly washed. Slip under the covers. Relax. If necessary, rethink the events of the day until you grow drowsy. Ask for a divine dream once again, just before dropping off.

Assume a Ritual Sleep Posture

Some ancient writers, in describing dream incubatory temples, made passing references to the specialized "sleep postures" that were apparently in use by those who were undergoing temple sleep.

Much research has failed to uncover explicit instructions regarding this somewhat unusual aspect of sacred sleep. The only clue that I've found is contained in the Egyptian Bes spell (Chapter 2), in which a black cloth is wound around one hand, and, once in bed, the other end is wrapped around the neck. This would certainly create an unusual posture, depending on the length of cloth left stretched between the hand and the neck.

The rationale for sleep postures seems clear: like the fasting, special diets, and herbal concoctions that were given to the supplicants to ensure a divine dream, assuming a specific posture before sleep firmly impressed in the mind the uniqueness of this form of sleep. Even in sleep, the supplicant would be performing a ritual.

Change is the most important aspect of postures during sacred sleep. The manner in which you rest in bed at night should not be your normal position. If you usually stretch out on your back, try your side. If you cross your hands on your chest, refrain from doing so. (Indeed: crossed hands seem to indicate an unwillingness to receive dream information.)

This change should not be so great that it prevents you from falling asleep. Too, you'll probably awaken in your old posture; this is no cause for alarm. If you simply can't sleep in unusual postures, don't worry: it shouldn't affect your sacred sleep.

I've found that an ideal posture is to lie on my back with my arms stretched out over my head (not crossed behind it). Admittedly, this can be difficult on a short bed, but it is what works best for me. This sacred posture (which is completely different from my normal bedtime posture) represents my willingness to receive dream messages. It is also a supplicatory pose: I'm stretching my arms toward the deity. You may wish to try this posture, or create your own unique forms.

Sleep

Allow yourself to naturally fall asleep, certain that your prayer will be answered. And, finally, dream.

DREAM

A Suggested Dream Ritual

Bathe in salted water. Dry yourself and dress in appropriate garments. Create your altar (if necessary). Go before it with your offering. Light the candles and incense (if used). Place your offering in the bowl while saying:

> *Isis* (insert your Messenger's name here)
> *Goddess of magic* (insert an attribute here)
> *Creatrix of divine dreams* (or Creator)
> *Accept this, my offering.*

Direct your attention to the divinity's image. Close your eyes. Breathe deeply. Raise your hands in supplication to the deity image. Open your eyes and begin your prayer (inserting the appropriate term where indicated):

> *Isis-of-the-Moon* (your deity's name),
> *Divine Lover of Osiris* (aspect),
> *Protectress of the weak* (attribute),
> *Enthroned One of the sacred sistrum*
>   (symbol)

Hear the prayer of Your worshipper!
  (general request),
Lady of the Fragrant Lotus (symbol),
Queen of Egypt (aspect),
Before Whom the stars bow in allegiance
  (praise),
You Who rises as Sirius (symbol),
Who floods the Nile (attribute),
Isis . . . (your deity's name),
Mistress of all Magics, (attribute)
Bringer of love, (attribute)
Hear the prayer of Your worshipper!
  (general request),
Stand beside me this night (general
  request),
Appear in my dreams, Great Counsellor!
  (general request),
Come to Your worshipper in the night
  (general request),
Bearing a true dream, a divine dream
  (general request),
Come to me, Queen of Stars! (attribute),
Answer my prayer (general request).

Here state your question: "Should I move?"
"What can I do to enhance my spirituality?" "Is
this job offer suitable?" and so on.

Great Goddess of the Moon
_____ (symbol),
Send me a dream! (general request),
All praises to You! (general request).

Stand for a few moments before the deity's image. Lower your arms, extinguish the candles and incense, and go to bed. Assume a ritual sleep posture, sleep and dream.

In times of great stress, or when circumstances simply don't allow you to perform a complete dream ritual, an abbreviated form may be helpful. Purify yourself. Get into bed. Whisper a short prayer, something like the following:

Isis (your deity's name),
Hear the prayer of Your worshipper.
Reveal Yourself to me in a dream.
Send me a dream in the night.
Answer my prayer:

Here state your question.

All praises to You,
Great Isis! (your deity's name).

Such short rituals may be necessary when sharing a bedroom (or a bed), during travel away from home, and under other circumstances.

Chapter 12

Dream rituals are an integral part of sacred sleep. Create your rite with reverence, power, and emotional involvement, and it should succeed.

III

DAWN

Chapter 13

RECALLING AND RECORDING YOUR DREAMS

R ays of golden light intrude into the world of blues and purples and silvers. The conscious mind unfurls itself from its rest. The body, freed once again from the imprisoning effects of sleep, flexes and moves. The eyes flicker, then open. A yawn. A stretch. Dream time is over.

Waking is the moment of greatest importance to all who would work with dreams. During these fleeting seconds, our psychic minds transfer to our conscious minds a fairly clear and comprehensive memory of the previous night's dreams. Each moment that elapses after waking allows the conscious mind to twist or to distort the dream. Indeed, in as little as fifteen minutes we may experience difficulty remembering even one detail of one dream.

This being the case, it's necessary to record all dreams immediately upon waking. The sooner this is done, the greater the accuracy and scope of the recording and, thus, the greater potential that we'll be able to utilize the information contained within the dream.

Recording dreams experienced during sacred sleep is profoundly more important, for the words of the deities should not be lightly forgotten. If we've spent the previous night in purification and ritual, we can certainly spend the first few moments of the new day recording the results of our preparations. The recording of our dreams is the next step of sacred sleep: a continuation of the larger ritual.

A Dream Diary

The most efficient means of recording dreams yet found is the utilization of a dream diary. This may be any diary or blank, bound book. Even a spiral-bound notebook will suffice. (A few books designed for use as dream diaries are on the market. Most are filled with illustrations and quotations that may distract you from your real purpose: recalling and recording the dreams. Blank books produce the best results.)

Keep the diary and a pen on a table beside your bed. If you wear glasses, place them beneath the diary before sleep, so that in the morning you'll have to first touch the diary before securing your lenses. You may also wish to place a small flashlight beside the diary (for recording dreams if you wake in the night).

Upon waking, don't leave your bed. Lie still for a moment and mentally run through the dreams you've just had. Then begin writing. Don't think about what you're writing; record your dreams.

At the top of the page, write the date (3/19/92 takes less time than does writing March 19, 1992). Immediately begin to record your dream. If you can't recall everything about it, record what you do remember. If there were several segments to the dream, you needn't record them in the proper order. Simply write down everything that you can recall.

What should you record? Events. Sights of your Messenger. Words from your Messenger. Words stated by others (by whom and to whom). Words that you yourself have spoken. Persons whom you know and strangers. Colors. Smells. Sounds. Tastes. Thoughts. Your emotional state. Symbols (cups, animals, numbers). The time of day. Seasons. Physical feelings. Many of these may play a part in your dreams. Don't dwell solely on the visual aspects; record everything that you can remember about the dream, down to the last detail. Avoid evaluating the points of a dream that seem to be the most important and writing down only these.

After you've recorded your dream, read through it. If you've forgotten something, add it to your recitation. If you suddenly remember the correct order in which certain events occurred, rewrite the main points of the dream below your original entry in the appropriate order—don't cross out your original entry, for the first symbols or events that you've consciously recalled may bear the greatest significance.

BLOCKED DREAMS

At times we simply can't remember our dreams. When this occurs, date the page and write "no recall." Spend a few moments attempting to determine why you have no recall.

Dreams of all types may be blocked by emotional problems, certain forms of illness, stress, poor diet and prescription drugs. Additionally, waking to an alarm clock may also thrust the dream from your conscious mind.

A lack of dream recall after sacred sleep deserves serious examination, for it should produce remembered dreams. Was your question explicit? Was it the correct question? Are you afraid of the possible answer? (This can easily be the root cause.) Have you ignored advice given in previous divine dreams? Have you recently questioned your Messenger's ability to dispense wisdom? Answering such questions may well lead to the reason for your lack of recall of a divine dream.

The most likely culprit for unremembered dreams is the conscious mind itself. This half of our consciousness, which happily censors out psychic information on a daily basis, may also censor dreams that, it is convinced, may "harm" us. It may decide that the Messenger's advice is too advanced, too scary, too revolutionary for us to handle. Sacred sleep is, ideally, a cooperative process between the psychic and the conscious minds. Unfortunately, the latter easily has the upper hand during those few seconds when we awaken.

If you believe that this is occurring, say the following words each night, after your ritual, as you get into bed:

> *I will remember my dreams, both positive*
> *and negative. I'm not frightened by my*
> *dreams. Nothing can keep me from remem-*
> *bering them. I'm prepared for the truth.*

(Say this only if you are, indeed, prepared for the truth.) This should prove to be effective after a few nights.

Divine messages lost in unremembered dreams received during sacred sleep can be regained by asking the same question on a subsequent night. The deities have always been willing to speak on the same subject on at least two occasions.

REMEMBERING DREAMS

Some specific techniques have been found to enhance the ability to remember our dreams. The easiest of these is to spend a great deal of time thinking about them. Read books. Look through your dream diary each night. Talk to others about your dreams, and ask to hear their nighttime experiences. Work on your personal dream book (see Chapter 14). Realize that many dreams occur every night, whether we remember them or not. Familiarize your conscious mind with the realm of dreams. Teach it that the dream world is just as important as the waking world.

The theory underlying these techniques is that the conscious mind, flooded with so much dream information, will eventually relent from censoring our dreams. The more familiar the conscious mind becomes with dreams and their symbols (the language of dreams), the more willing it will be to allow us to remember them.

Most of us have met people who claim that they never dream. This is apparently untrue, for dreams are a natural part of the human experience. These people have become experts at blocking all dreams, and thus have convinced themselves that they don't have them. If you are one of these people, retrain your conscious mind to accept dreams.

Writing down our divine dreams is nothing less than recording the words of the divine beings Who guide our lives. As such, it is an important spiritual task of those who would engage in sacred sleep.

Chapter 14

Dream Interpretation

As we have seen, dream interpretation is an intensely personal art. It is the vital next step of sacred sleep. So, too, is identifying significant dreams. This and the following chapter provide guidance in determining the messages of your dreams. The work may at first seem daunting. Soon, however, you'll discover it to be an infinitely rewarding part of your life.

Types of Dreams

We examined several types of dreams in Chapter 1. Here, for easy reference, I'll summarize this information and provide tips on determining the nature of your dreams.

Natural Dreams

These are fanciful dreams, wish-fulfillment dreams, or rehashes of the day's events; scenes from movies or television programs that you've recently seen; bits of books and magazine articles; recent positive or negative events that return to haunt you. Such dreams hardly need to be analyzed. However, they should be recorded in your dream diary.

Every dream—even those obtained during sacred sleep—does not bear a profound message. Sometimes our deities can't immediately answer us, and natural dreams can occur on the same night as divine dreams. Some dreams are little more than the mind expanding on waking activities during the night. Natural dreams can be easily identified by the events and characters that occur within them.

Memories of Astral Projection

Most ancient cultures accepted the concept that, during sleep, the human soul escaped the body and traveled at will throughout time and space. This phenomenon is known in western occultism as astral projection (or "soul travel").

Dreams based on memories of astral projection may include visits to alternate planes of existence, flying, the sighting of ancient temples, unearthly scenes. They are of fantastic, unusual natures, unrelated to our everyday lives.

Astral projection memories (in the form of dreams) are quite common in childhood. Most adults lose this ability as they mature, although some continue to consciously remember astral projection.

To determine whether a dream is actually a remembrance of an astral journey, analyze its emotional content, symbols, location, and other factors. Keep in mind that the astral realm is often referred to as "the plane of illusion," and such dreams can't always be regarded as significant.

Telepathic Dreams

Messages from other persons received in dreams should be quite clear and require no interpretation. You may, however, wish to call the person on the following morning and ask, "What's up?"

Prophetic Dreams

Prophetic dreams are delivered by our personal deities. They contain messages concerning our immediate futures and, indeed, are divine dreams.

Psychic Dreams

Psychic dreams differ from prophetic dreams, for the source of the information is our subconscious mind. These dreams relate to possible future events in either symbolic or lucidly clear form. During sleep, this psychic information is easily placed into the form of a dream.

Most dreams of this type tend to be negative, but some are positive. A few wish-fulfillment dreams may masquerade as psychic dreams. After you've correctly identified several psychic dreams (which will be proven by the future), you'll recognize their nature. Such dreams should be carefully analyzed to discover their underlying messages.

Divinely Inspired Dreams

These are just that—sent by the Messengers for a specific purpose. These can arrive unbidden or during sacred sleep. They may include warnings, advice, messages of comfort or answers to specific questions. To determine whether a dream is of divine inspiration, see Chapter 15.

Serial Dreams

We've all had these. Most "dreams" actually consist of a series of episodes. Any combination of the above dreams may be consecutively experienced in a single night. Thus, you may have a wish-fulfillment dream, a psychic dream, and a dream containing a message from a deity in the same night.

Separate dreams occurring during one evening may or may not be linked. Consider serial dreams, both individually and collectively.

PERSONAL DREAM INTERPRETATION

Of the above types of dreams, only prophetic, psychic, and divine dreams need to be analyzed, though the below information can be used for all types of dreams. This is my personal dream interpretation plan:

1. Begin soon after recording your dream

2. Determine the dream type

3. Make a list of the dream's symbols

4. Consult your personal dream book

5. Unlock the dream's message

Begin Soon After Recording Your Dream

It's best not to delay in interpreting your dream. Analyzing its message while the dream is still fresh in your mind may well provide additional insight.

Determine the Dream Type

Based on this, determine whether the dream should be interpreted. Some dreams have no need of interpretation. They are what the Hawaiians term "clear" or "straight up." Only symbolically complex dreams require interpretation.

Make a List of the Dream's Symbols

Study every aspect of the dream to reveal its symbols and inner nature. Make a list of the important symbols, on a separate piece of paper from your dream diary, in the order in which they were received within the dream. Include dream actions, words, incidents, and persons, but also include the following:

Emotional Tone: Was the dream joyous? Peaceful? Contemplative? Exciting? Frightening? Uplifting? Refreshing? Stressful? Spiritual? Secretive? Determining the dream's emotional tone (whether it was positive or negative, regardless of the activities that occurred within it) can have a great bearing on the dream's interpretation.

Location: In a home? A temple? In a field of grass? In the desert? At sea? Beside a river, spring, or well? In a cave? In a public place? Was the place known to you? Unknown? Domestic? Foreign? Have you visited the location in waking consciousness, or only in dreams? Did there seem to be no location? (If so, any symbols that did appear may be of great significance.) The location may or may not have an effect on the dream's interpretation. The most profound symbolic messages have been received in the most unlikely of dream locations.

Time of Day and Celestial Phenomena: Was it dawn? Morning? Day? Dusk? Night? Was the moon visible? If so, which phase? Was there an eclipse? If so, was it solar or lunar? Did you see rainbows? Lunar rainbows? Northern Lights? Fireballs?

Elemental Forces: Was it raining? Pouring? Storming? Sunny? Cloudy? Snowing? Foggy? Misty? Icy? Windy? Did dew cover the plants? Did lightning flash through the sky? Did you hear thunder? Was is humid? Dry? Cold? Hot? Were there earthquakes? Floods? Hurricanes? Typhoons?

Your Personal State: This should also be taken into account. Your health, emotions, relationships, finances may well dramatically affect the dream's interpretation.

Other Symbols: Record all symbols present in the dream: words, actions, activities, trees, plants, flowers, animals, birds, foods, water, liquids, fires (destructive or warming), blood, numbers, circles, geometric figures, stones, colors, mountains, caves, towers, winged beings and a host of other important symbols (see Appendix 1). Deliberate movements from right to left or left to right (your own or those of animals or others) should also be recorded. In essence, everything that is seen, heard, or that occurs during a dream is a dream symbol.

Consult Your Personal Dream Book

As discussed in Chapter 8, most published dream books are of little use. However, some catalogue of dream interpretations would be of tremendous value when beginning to decode the messages of the night. This would, ideally, be a collection of personal symbols related to religion, spiritual practices, profession, habits, life patterns, relationship status, past experiences and so on. Since we place highly individual meanings on these symbols, we should create our own dream books.

CREATING YOUR DREAM BOOK

This is a simple process. Buy a loose-leaf notebook (one in which you can rearrange the order of the pages), and fill it with 100 pages of paper. To make your first entry, think of a symbol that has a powerful, personal impact and that frequently appears in your dreams.

Record this symbol at the top of the page in large letters. Quickly write the first associations that come into your mind while looking at the symbol. Don't censor, write! (Limit each association to one or two words.)

Use one page for each subject, and keep the pages in alphabetical order. Add pages with new symbols as you have the time or inclination. Eventually, you may discover that the recording of your dream symbols and their associations is an illuminating adventure into self-discovery.

Be explicit and concise. Don't censor, don't lie, and don't write what you "think" you should write. If the sea represents a womb to you, record it as such. If you're in an abusive relationship, don't record "happiness," "love," and "caring" under Marriage (and exit from the relationship as quickly as possible). If you connect hospitals with death rather than with healing, medicine, cleanliness, and rest, state so.

Just a few of the important symbols that you may wish to interpret in your dream book include those listed earlier under "Other Symbols." Also include all symbols directly related to your personal deity (see Chapter 10 and Appendix 1).

At first, the task of recording hundreds of symbols and their meanings may seem quite daunting, but it is precisely the reverse. Writing one word at the top of a page and following it with the first ten or so words that pop into your mind in relation to this word shouldn't require more than fifteen minutes, tops. Spending one-quarter of an hour each day on this project will allow you to quickly create your dream book; within a year you'll have over 300 pages, and you'll soon need to buy another notebook.

You may experience some difficulty in determining the meanings of certain symbols while creating your dream book. You may never have consciously thought about animals, colors, and objects in symbolic ways. This is fine. If the information is necessary, you'll eventually retrieve it from your subconscious mind.

Your first entry may resemble the following:

> *BLUE*
> *Ocean, emotions, travel, dolphins, seasick-*
> *ness, depths, subconscious mind, psychic*
> *awareness, Aphrodite, boats, purification,*
> *salt.*

The first associations that you record will be among your most potent dream symbols. The others may well never point to the inherent meaning of a dream. This is true because when we record our symbolic associations, the conscious mind soon intrudes and replaces subconscious associations with conscious ones.

If this exercise is continued on a regular basis, you'll compile a comprehensive collection of dream symbols and their potential meanings. This book is the most valuable that you can own. It's not only a record, it's a part of you, pulled from the deepest levels of your subconscious mind and brought into the light of day to assist your life.

Our dream books are intimately personal records of our symbolic language. As such they should be treated with respect and hidden from the eyes of others, even mates, unless you wish to share every single aspect of your being.

Consult Your Dream Book

Look up the dream's symbols in your dream book. Study the associations listed there and determine if they are of significance within the dream (see below). Consulting even personal dream books is not simply a matter of looking up a symbol—all symbols must be viewed within the larger context of the dream.

Unlock the Dream's Overall Message

You now have a wealth of information before you. It's time to piece it together, like a puzzle, to determine the dream's larger picture. Here are some hints.

Compare All Symbols: I mean all symbols, from the most insignificant to the most outstanding. Compare them. Search for connections (major symbols should tell a story of some kind). Study the associations in your dream book. Take into account everything that we've discussed above.

Rely on Your Intuition: Intuition can be an invaluable ally in dream interpretation. Our subconscious (psychic) minds are, after all, the originators of all nondivine dreams. We should listen if they speak during interpretation. They may well point us to the last piece of the puzzle.

Resist Blocking a Dream's Message: Don't fight this process; work with it. Consider it to be an adventure of discovery. Put on your best Sherlock Holmes cap and allow the dream's message to become clear. If you begin to see something that frightens you, close your eyes, breathe deeply for a few moments, then forge ahead. You may think that you'll never unlock a specific dream's meaning. Relax and begin again.

Write Out Your Interpretation: You can do this either in your dream diary, directly under the dream, or in a separate book kept solely for this purpose. Make this as explicit as possible.

Example of Dream Interpretation

I recently had a dream that may serve as an example of this interpretive process. Following is my recording of the dream, made at about 6:30 A.M. on Wednesday, March 18, 1992:

Day, on a grassy plain. Sunshiny and warm. I felt wonderful. I was watching a group of women who were creating some type of large, wreath-like structures with dried, golden yet pliable grass. Men and women would step through these structures. The big secret was that no one was supposed to know that they'd been made by women—or of what they were made. Later, I watched these women create ovoid objects of incredibly fine weave with this same material by spinning the "grass" with great rapidity between their hands to form various objects.

Here's the list of symbols that I compiled from this short dream:

Day
Outdoors on a grassy plain
Sunshine
Warm
Pleasant, uplifting emotions
Circle
Grass
Spinning
Women dominant in dream's action
"Stepping through" motif
Secrecy

I was immediately aware, after studying the dream and its important aspects, that this was of great importance. The following interpretation is happily subjective, but I've chosen to use the third person in relating it here:

> *This person is very creative (spinning). Much of his creation is concerned with spirituality (circle, secrecy). Though this work has been quite fulfilling to this person (happiness), he will soon be entering into a new phase of this work (stepping through the circle of grass). The large number of women present*

*in the dream may be indicative of a number
of things:*

*a. The person's creativity emerges from
the psychic mind (traditionally considered to
be female)*

*b. The person is involved in Goddess
worship, and/or*

*c. The dream was sent by a Goddess
(spinning is a familiar goddess symbol).*

*The overall interpretation of this dream
seems to be: "You will soon enter a new
realm of consciousness or will find a new
focus of religious expression. "*

Dream interpretation can be incredibly simple—
as long as we limit this practice to our own dreams.
Interpreting the dreams of others is difficult unless
a psychic link is established between the dreamer
and the interpreter. It isn't recommended.

With experience comes confidence. Analyzing
dreams will soon be as easy as opening your eyes in
the morning, and you may well wonder why you
waited so long to begin.

Chapter 15

DIVINE DREAMS

In Chapter 14, I outlined a system for inter-preting important dreams. I purposefully delayed discussion of the interpretation of divine dreams until the present chapter, for such dreams must be addressed in a most singu-lar manner. Dreams provided to us by our per-sonal deities require the greatest attention.

WHY SHOULD DIVINE DREAMS BE OBSCURE?

Our personal deities may send us puzzling dreams for a number of reasons. Perhaps the most important of these reasons is that we're more likely to ponder an obscure dream than one requiring little interpretation. This period of conscious thought may well impress the dream's importance on us, encouraging us to act on its message. We realize that there are many ways to express ourselves, and sometimes the indirect approach is the most effective. The deities seem to favor this approach.

Unfamiliarity with the Messenger's symbols and attributes may obscure an otherwise clear dream. The divinity certainly can't be faulted for speaking in her or his own symbolic language. When we're knowledgeable concerning the attributes of our Messengers, such dreams lose much of their obscurity.

Additionally, keep in mind that many deities were once worshipped in great mystery rituals. The nature of these mysteries (such as the Eleusinian rites) is still unknown, for vows of secrecy forbade the worshippers from revealing them to outsiders. However, we do know that these rites were steeped in symbolic actions and invocations. Many of these took place within the most sacred precincts of the temples. If the deities enjoyed such symbolic rites in the past, They certainly may continue to utilize similar forms in communicating with their worshippers. Be prepared for the revelation of great mysteries if Demeter hands you a stalk of grain.

RECOGNIZING DIVINE DREAMS

Look for the following when determining if a dream was of divine inspiration.

The Messenger Appears in Her or His Usual Form

The Messenger appears in the manner in which we normally visualize her or him. No words may be spoken. Such dreams are obviously divine. If a woman appears to a worshipper of Diana dressed in a white chiton, standing on the moon and shooting arrows into the stars, there can be little doubt that this is Diana Herself, and that this is a divine dream.

The Messenger Appears in Symbolic Form

The Diana worshipper mentioned above may have a dream that includes, among other symbols, a white dog, an arrow, a forest and moonlight. Her presence in the dream may not be as easily determined if these clues are recognized as divine symbols, so such dreams require careful study.

Realize that divine symbols may not seem to have extraordinary importance within the context of the dream itself. During a seemingly ordinary dream you may be handed a piece of bread. To a worshipper of Demeter, this will be the only clue of Her presence.

Be alert to both ancient and modern forms of divine symbols. Chariots may be seen as cars; clay tablets as books and computers; flying in an airplane may be connected with a winged deity, and so on.

The Messenger Speaks Directly to You

The deity may say, in human voice, "Despair not. You will soon be loved." "You are already pregnant, though you do not yet know this." "Find another love." "Mix honey with water and take twice a day." "The position will give you great wealth." These dreams require no interpretation and are unquestionably of divine inspiration. Though rare, they do occur. You may not be able to see your deity, but hearing such words may be evidence enough.

A Deity Related to Your Messenger Appears

Some deities will send others to answer our questions, or more than one deity may appear. This may necessitate knowledge of the deities' familial relationships. The absence of your specific Messenger in a dream doesn't indicate that it wasn't of divine origin.

The Dream Was Received During Sacred Sleep

Not every dream that we experience during sacred sleep is divine, but at least one is usually of divine origin. Those that are received during sacred sleep have an edge over those that occurred at other times.

The Dream Is Related to Your Question or Request

This can be difficult to answer until you've interpreted its message. However, your intuition may make you aware that your dream is indeed related to your question. If two or more of these factors are true, there can be little doubt that you've experienced a divinely inspired dream.

Interpreting Divine Dreams

Unlocking the meaning of divine dreams is a tricky process. Our conscious minds are predisposed to dismiss dreams of great importance. Any suggestion that a dream may have been delivered to us by our Messenger can set off sirens and flashing red lights in our waking consciousness: "Danger! Danger! This dream really means something! Better block it or make its message difficult to read."

This exaggeration has been necessary to make a point: the conscious mind can have difficulty in coping with divine dreams. We may be the most spiritual, religiously active persons on earth, yet our waking minds can still bear shadowed corners of socially created doubt.

If you experience this problem, it might be overcome by retraining your conscious mind. Let it know that you know what you're doing. Assuage its doubts by repeating specific statements every morning before you begin to interpret your dreams:

> *This dream is important to us.*
> *This dream can assist us.*
> *I want no interference.*

You needn't feel silly speaking to your mind. You have talked to it (and trained it) throughout your entire life. Repeat this statement, then get down to the work of unlocking the dream's message.

1. Was the dream's overall tone that of warning? Of impending danger? Of peace? Comfort? Excitement? (This may determine whether the dream was positive or negative.)

2. What is the dream's basic form? Revelatory? Instructive? Educational? (This may determine whether the dream was prophetic or simply informational.)

3. What was your emotional state during the dream?

4. Which dream actions are directly related to your Messenger? (Some parts of dreams may not be of importance, or may be of lesser importance. This can usually be determined by the context in which they take place.)

5. Were you handed anything in the dream by your Messenger. If so, what was this object? (These symbols represent powerful connections with your personal deity, and may be the heart of the dream's message.)

6. Was any object specifically pointed out to you? A drawing, painting, an animal? If so, did you gain an understanding of the object thus seen? (Such symbols may also be of great importance.)

Once these questions have been answered, make a list of the dream's most important symbols (as described in Chapter 14). Don't limit this to only those symbols that you believe are divinely related to your dream; list them all, in the order in which they occurred. Consult your personal dream book for insight into these symbols. (See Chapter 14.)

Now, finally, compare the dream's content with your dream question. Examine the symbols. Are there any obvious or subtle connections between your question and the dream? If you inquired about a job, do symbols of employment appear? If so, are they presented in a positive or negative light?

Following these steps should allow you to extract a divine dream's message. If difficulties arise, overcome them with your intuition, and trust yourself.

A Few Examples

I recently had a dream in which I picked up a book that was of immense interest to me. I flipped through the pages and was quite thrilled with the subject matter (which was written in English), but, upon closer inspection, I realized that the book contained only masses of jumbled, incoherent information. I also looked hard at the price, which was written in pencil and said "URI100RUR." I read this (within the dream) as the book's price tag: $100.

During interpretation the following morning, I realized that this was a divine dream. A goddess (probably Nisaba, the Sumerian goddess of writing and wisdom) was informing me that the book on which I was laboring lacked structure and contained too much information. The letters that I saw on the inside front cover twice (or, perhaps, thrice) spelled the word Ur (an ancient Sumerian city-state). The high price tag was indicative of this dream's great importance, and the fact that it was written in pencil I easily equated with the stylus used for writing cuneiform in ancient Sumer.

This was a short dream, but it made a great impression. It was also sandwiched between several other dreams. If I hadn't been alert to searching for clues, I might have missed this goddess' message (which was quite helpful—and absolutely correct). In another recent dream, a door appeared on my messy living room floor. I equated the door with keys, and therefore with Gaea. (Gaea is the ancient goddess of the earth Who is today associated with ecology. Her name is increasingly being used to refer to the Earth Herself as a living, sentient being.) I realized that this dream was a hint from Gaea to clean my house. This example should make it plain that even divine dreams aren't always concerned with shattering predictions or major problems; they can also be gentle reminders.

CHALLENGES

Dreams that Bear No Direct Relation to Your Question

There may be mornings on which you can find little or no connection between your dream and your dream question. If you're certain of the dream's divine nature, consider the possibility that you've received a message concerning a more pressing matter. Such dreams are usually quite significant. Our personal deities can send us other dreams than those that we've requested if they're of greater importance. Repeat your dream question on another night.

Doubt

If you're unsure that you've successfully decoded your divine dream, repeat the question on a successive night and explain that you've had trouble understanding the message. A new, clearer dream may be presented to you.

Using Divine Dreams

In Chapter 9, I briefly mentioned the importance of actually using the information received during sacred sleep. Asking a divine being for advice is far different from asking a friend. A friend can convey her or his feelings, recite knowledge about the subject, or relate past experiences. The Goddess (or the God), however, is the possessor of all wisdom. Fully following Her advice is likely to prove quite fruitful. Following it only half-way will be less so. Ignoring it, "forgetting" it, or claiming to be too busy to incorporate its message will accomplish nothing.

You may receive the same divine dream on several occasions for a number of reasons:

+ The dream wasn't recognized as divine

+ The dreamer was awakened before the dream's completion

✦ The dream was forgotten before it was recorded

✦ The dreamer made an inaccurate (or incomplete) record

✦ The dreamer inaccurately interpreted the dream

✦ The dreamer didn't act upon the message

Asking for a dream gives us the responsibility to utilize its advice. We may have many excuses for failing to do this: fear of change, doubt, or a busy schedule. Such reasons can certainly seem quite compelling. If you don't know what to do, if you doubt the wisdom of your possible future actions, or are frightened of change, ask for another divine dream during sacred sleep. This may well soothe your worries and more sharply define your course of action.

Recognizing divine dreams, extracting their messages, and acting upon their advice are integral aspects of sacred sleep.

Chapter 16

SACRED DREAMING

I am aware that some of you, having read this far, are recalling dreams in which your personal deity has spontaneously appeared. I'm equally aware that some of you must think me quite mad. This is, perhaps, understandable, since the realm of dreams operates within a variant reality that appears only when we sleep. The phenomenon of dreaming cannot be viewed within the framework of waking consciousness.

Dream reality is a state between our world and the stars, between earth and sky, between the human experience and the goddesses and gods. Within its unlimited space, divine advice, prophetic messages, and comfort can be acquired through direct communication, unhampered by the restraints of our waking reality.

Dreams won't soon lose their mysterious qualities. Sleep researchers will never discover the secrets of dreams merely by studying the body and the brain, for many dreams stem from aspects of ourselves that possess no physically measurable dimensions, while others emerge from higher sources.

Those visions that come to us in the night can have a tremendous impact on our waking lives. Indeed: knowledge acquired during sacred sleep is meant to be used. It's presented to us for the purpose of improving our lives. Though we needn't exclusively base our daily existences on our divine dreams, we can certainly utilize this wisdom and would be unwise to omit so doing.

Our busy lives leave us with precious little time to engage in spiritual activities. We may allow the many demands placed on us during our waking hours to take precedence over our more important goals of spiritual development. In this rush, we may lose touch with our deities.

Sacred sleep, however, requires little more than a bath, a short ritual, and sleep. Utilizing our nightly periods of rest to contact our goddesses and gods is a refreshingly ancient method of enhancing our spiritual lives.

Once you embark on this journey, you may soon find that the preparations and rituals are unnecessary, and that your deity (or deities) will appear in your dreams as needed to offer you advice and counselling. When this occurs, you can be assured that sacred sleep has become an important part of your life, that your deity has heard, and that she or he will continue to respond in the future.

Our deities are independent supreme beings, possessing wisdom, personality, and great influences. It is only fitting that, in times of difficulty, we ask them to lend us Their power and wisdom.

Chapter 16

The deities await our calls. Sleep opens the gates
to their temples and allows them to approach us. . . .

> *Lay your burdens upon Us,*
> *We who know the past and future,*
> *Who possess all wisdom and insight,*
> *Who care for Our worshippers.*
> *We shall send you visions in the night,*
> *Divine dreams of understanding and*
> *Compassion, knowledge and advice.*
> *Call to Us and We shall appear in your*
>   *dreams.*
> *Sleep is the sacred rite of Our worship;*
> *Dreams are Our utterances.*
> *Call to Us through the starry eve!*
> *Call to Us!*
> *Call to US!*

A Catalogue of Sacred Dream Symbols

This catalogue lists symbols, physical phenomena, and attributes that may appear in dreams, and that may betoken your Messenger's (corresponding deity) presence in the dream. No "meanings" are given here—only the symbols and their representative deities. This appendix has been designed to quickly ascertain deities associated with specific symbols.

Animals (Protection of): Artemis

Ankh: Isis

Antares (Star): Isis

Antelope: Set

Anvil: Hesphaestus, Vulcan

Apple: Aphrodite, Eris, Hera, Pomona

April: Aphrodite

Armor: Athena

Aquarius (Constellation): Ea

Arrow: Amor, Aphrodite, Artemis, Eros

Axe (see also *Pickaxe):* Adad

Barley: Demeter, Nisaba

Bay (Laurel): Apollo, Artemis

Bee: Demeter, Zeus

Beer: Demeter, Geshtinanna, Isis, Ninkasi

Birth: Artemis, Heket, Hera, Juno

Blue: Nut

Boat: Sin

Box: Persephone

*Bow (*see also *Arrow):* Amor, Artemis, Diana, Eros, Inanna, Ishtar

Bowl: Hygeia, Salus

Bread: Ceres, Demeter, Isis, Ninkasi

Bridle: Athena

Bull: Adad, Anu, Apis, Mars, Serapis, Zeus

Business: Mercury

Caduceus: Aesculapius, Asklepios

Calendar: Sin, Thoth

*Cap, White (*see also *Hat):* Jupiter

Cat: Bast, Isis, Sekhmet

Cave: Demeter

Chariot: Aphrodite, Hera, Jupiter, Poseidon, Selene

Clay Tablets: Marduk, Nabu

Competitions: Aphrodite, Eris, Hermes

Contents: Aphrodite, Eris, Hermes

Copper: Ea

Cornucopia: Fortuna, Gaea, Tyche

Cow: Diana, Faunus, Hathor, Hera, Lathar, Nut

Cow Horns: Hathor, Isis

Crescent: Diana, Sin

Crescent Moon: Diana, Sin

Crocodile: Set

Crook: Osiris

Crossroads: Hecate

Cuckoo Bird: Zeus

Cypress: Adad

Date Palm Tree: Hathor

Dates (Food): Hathor

Deer: Artemis

Dew: Zeus

Diadem: Anu, Hera

Dilgan (Star): Ea

Dog: Asklepios, Anubis, Artemis, Diana, Gula, Hecate, Inanna, Ishtar, Isis, Ninurta

Dolphin: Poseidon

Donkey: Vesta

Door: Janus, Juno

Dove: Aphrodite, Ishtar

Dragon: Marduk

Dwarf: Bes

Eagle: Zeus

Earthquake: Poseidon

Eight: Inanna, Ishtar

Eight-pointed Star: Ishtar:

Eye: Horus

Falcon: Ra, Ra-Harakty

Fifteen: Ishtar

Fifty: Ningirsu

Fig: Dionysius

Fire: Hephaestus, Hestia, Vesta

Fireplace: Hestia, Vesta

Fish: Aphrodite

Five: Minerva

Flail: Osiris

Flint: Jupiter

Flute: Hermes, Pan

Flowers: Ceres, Flora

Food (in general): Demeter

Forest: Diana, Pan

Forty: Ea

Frog: Heket

Fruit: Ceres, Gaea, Pomona

Garden: Aphrodite, Spes

Garments, Linen: Isis

Globe: Gaea, Tyche

Goat: Juno, Pan

Goat Skin: Bes

Goose: Amun, Geb

Grain: Ashnan, Ceres, Demeter, Flora, Hermes, Nisaba, Osiris, Persephone, Shala, Spes

Grape: Bacchus, Dionysius, Liber, Pan

Gymnastics: Hermes

Gypsum: Ninurta

Hair: Artemis

Hammer: Hephaestus, Vulcan

Hare: Osiris (as Onnophris)

Hat: Hermes

Hawk: Horus, Ra-Horakty

Hearth: Hestia, Vesta

Helmet: Aphrodite, Athena, Minerva

Herald's Staff: Hermes, Iris

Home: Hestia, Vesta

Horn: Hypnos

Horse: Poseidon

Horse Races: Poseidon

Hunting: Artemis, Diana, Inanna, Ishtar, Pan

Ibis: Thoth

Ivy: Bacchus, Dionysius

Jackal: Anubis

Jupiter (Planet): Marduk

Justice: Nanna, Shamash, Zeus

Key: Gaea, Hecate, Janus

Kite (Bird): Isis

Knife: Bes

Lance: Mars

Lead (Metal): Ninmah, Marduk

Lettuce: Min

Lighthouse: Isis

Lightning: Adad, Jupiter, Poseidon, Zeus

Linen Garments: Isis

Lion: Artemis, Bast, Inanna, Ishtar, Isis, Sekhmet, Shamash

Lotus (Water Lily): Isis

Luck: Fortuna, Hermes

Lyre: Apollo, Hermes

Marriage: Ceres, Gaea, Hera, Juno

Milk: Gatumdug, Hathor, Isis

Monkey: Hapi

Moon: Artemis, Diana, Hecate, Ishtar, Isis, Luna,: Nanna, Sin

Mountain: Adad, Enlil, Jupiter, Ninhursag

Myrtle: Aphrodite

Oak: Jupiter, Zeus

Nudity, Female: Aphrodite, Ishtar

Nudity, Male: Apollo, Bes, Eros, Min

Obelisk: Ra

Ocean (see *Sea*)

Olive: Athena, Minerva

Owl: Athena, Minerva

Palm: Thoth

Palm, Date: Hathor, Dumuzi

Pan Pipes: Pan

Peacock: Hera, Juno

Pebble: Jupiter

Phallus: Dionysius, Min

Pickaxe: Enlil

Pig: Demeter, Nut

Pillars: Hermes

Pine Cone: Bacchus, Demeter, Dionysius, Artemis, Demeter, Dumuzi, Flora, Ninhursag, Persephone, Pomona, Spes, Uttu

Pleiades, the: Enlil

Plow: Ashnan

Pomegranate: Hera, Persephone

Poplar, White: Zeus

Poppy: Aphrodite, Hypnos

*Quiver (*see also *Arrow, Bow):* Artemis, Ishtar

Rain: Adad, Jupiter, Zeus

Rainbow: Iris

Rake: Athena

Ram: Amon, Ea, Hermes

Raven: Apollo

Reeds: Inanna, Ninurta

Riches: Adad, Fortuna, Hermes, Isis, Mercury

Roads: Hermes

Rooster: Athena

Rose: Aphrodite

Rosette: Ishtar

Rudder: Fortuna, Isis, Tyche

Sandals: Hermes

Sailing: Isis, Poseidon

Saw: Shamash

Scales: Anubis

Scepter: Anu, Hera, Jupiter, Persephone

Scorpion: Selket

Sea: Aphrodite, Poseidon

Shield: Aphrodite, Athena, Mars, Minerva

Ship: Dionysius, Ra

Shoes, Winged: Hermes

Shovel: Marduk, Nabu

Shuttle (as tool of Isis weaving): Isis

Sickle: Marduk

Sistrum: Bast, Hathor, Isis

Six: Adad

Sixty: Anu

Snake: Aesculapius, Asklepios, Athena, Demeter, Hecate, Hygeia, Ishtar, Isis, Salus, Zeus

Snow: Zeus

Sow: Isis, Nut

Sparrow: Aphrodite

Sphinx: Hamarkis

Spinning: Aphrodite, Isis, Minerva, Uttu

Spring (Season): Flora

Staff: Hermes

Star: Ishtar

Star (8-pointed): Ishtar

Star (16-pointed): Ishtar

Stars (all): Anu, Enlil

Stones: Hermes

Storms: Adad, Jupiter, Poseidon, Zeus

Stylus: Nabu, Nisaba

Sun: Helios, Horus, Mithras, Osiris, Ra, Shamash,Utu

Swallow: Aphrodite

Swan: Aphrodite, Apollo, Zeus

Sycamore: Hathor

Tamarisk: Anu

Thirty: Sin

Throne: Isis

Thunder: Adad, Jupiter, Zeus

Torch: Amor, Dionysius, Hecate, Isis (Ptolemaic)

Treaties: Hermes

Trees (in general): Diana, Faunus, Hathor, Pan

Trident: Poseidon

Twenty: Shamash

Uraeus: Isis

Vapors: Gaea

Vegetables: Gaea

Veil: Hera

Venus (Planet): Aphrodite, Inanna, Ishtar

Vine: Bacchus, Dionysius, Geshtinanna

Voyage: Isis, Poseidon

Vulture: Nekhebet

War: Inanna, Ishtar, Jupiter, Mars, Sekhmet

Water (see also *Sea):* Ea, Enki

Weaving: Minerva, Isis, Uttu

Wheat: Ceres, Demeter, Isis

Wheel: Fortuna, Tyche

White: Jupiter

Wind: Enlil, Ishkur, Ninurta

Wind, Hot: Sekhmet

Wine: Bacchus, Dionysius, Gesthinanna, Liber,
‑Hathor, Isis, Set

Wings: Amor, Artemis, Eos, Eros, Hypnos,
Inanna, Ishtar

Wolf: Mars

Womb: Demeter, Hathor, Nut

Woodpecker: Mars

Writing: Nebo, Nisaba, Thoth

Appendix 2

Dream Deities

This appendix lists on the following pages some of the divinities that are specifically associated with dreams and with sleep, though all deities can appear in our dreams.

Less familiar deities and those not mentioned elsewhere in this work are followed by short descriptions; information concerning the others can be found in Chapter 10 or by consulting the Index.

Adad

Aesculapius

Amphiaruas (Greek god of dream oracles and divination; He healed during sleep and was worshipped prior to Asklepios)

Artemis

Asklepios

Athena

Bes

Fauna

Faunus

Geshtinanna (Mesopotamian goddess of dream interpretation)

Hamarkis (a form of Horus)

Hathor

Hera

Hermes (also the bringer of refreshing sleep)

Horus

Hypnos (bringer of sleep)

Imhotep

Ishtar

Isis

Marduk

Morpheus (Roman god of dreams and bringer of sleep)

Nanshe (Sumerian goddess of dream interpretation; "mother interpretress of dreams"; "prophetess of the divinities")

Ninsun

Pan

Phantasos (god of dreams when He appeared in dreams; son of Somnos; brother of Morpheus)

Ptah

Serapis

Set

Seti I

Shauskha (a Hittite goddess associated with Ishtar)

Sin

Shamash

Somnos (Roman god of sleep)

Thoth Ningirsu

Trophonius (Greek oracular dream deity)

Zakar (Babylonian; the "emissary" of the moon god, Sin)

Zeus

Appendix 3

Natural Sleep-Inducing Techniques

Many persons have difficulty sleeping. Insomnia is rampant throughout the world. The causes are varied: a lack of certain minerals; poor diet; the overuse (or nighttime use) of caffeine, chocolate, and other stimulants; muscular tension; emotional problems; fear; an uncomfortable bed; nighttime noises; too much light in the room; lack of exercise; and other factors.

A number of prescription drugs have been created to address the issue of sleeplessness. All are dangerous. Millions of Americans are addicted to prescription sleeping drugs that their doctors have prescribed for long-term use (though none should be taken for more than two to six weeks).

If you have trouble sleeping at night, don't turn to artificial and hazardous drugs. Many other techniques have been found to relax the body and mind to the point that natural, refreshing sleep can take place. (For serious, continuing insomnia, see a sleep disorder specialist.)

This appendix lists some techniques and herbs that facilitate sleep. (Do not attempt sacred sleep while under the influence of prescription sleeping drugs.)

Prayer
+ Pray to your messenger to bring deep and lasting sleep swiftly

Baths
+ Feel free to run your purification bath a bit warmer just before bed if you have difficulty falling asleep (or staying asleep through the night); warm water relaxes stiff muscles; hot

baths can be invigorating (which defeats the purpose of inducing sleep), so keep it warm; for further relaxation, add 5 drops genuine lavender essential oil to the bath once the tub has been filled

✦ Tie up any combination of the following herbs in a washcloth or a square of muslin and add to the bath while the water is running: camomile, sage, passionflower, lemon balm, lavender; soak (see also Aromatherapy below)

Diet

✦ Eat lettuce before retiring to bring on sleep

✦ Avoid invigorating foods such as black and green tea, coffee, fennel, ginger, guarana, onions, and peppers, as well as all spicy foods

✦ Foods heavy in sugar shouldn't be eaten directly before bed

✦ Add a few whole anise seeds to milk; heat until hot; drink directly before going to bed

✦ Eat turkey or fish for dinner.

✦ A spoonful of honey before bed may bring on sleep

Herb Teas

+ Pour 1 cup boiling water over 1 tbsp. dried catnip; steep; drink before bed.

+ Pour 1 cup boiling water over 1 tbsp. dried camomile; steep; drink before bed.

+ Mix equal parts of scullcap and lady's slipper; add a dash of valerian; place 1 tbsp. of this mixture in a cup; pour 1 cup boiling water over the herbs; allow to steep, covered; hold your nose and drink (warning: this mixture doesn't smell or taste very good)

Pillows

+ Place a few drops of genuine lavender essential oil on your pillowcase directly before sleep

+ Make a small square of muslin. Mix ½ cup each of the following dried herbs: lemon balm, lavender, hops; stitch shut the pillow; place it beneath your pillow (or beside your head, if you use no pillow) and allow its fragrance to gently lull you to sleep

+ Try sleeping on a similar pillow filled with bran, as was the custom in ancient China.

Aromatherapy

✦ Essential oils that are conducive to sleep include lavender, chamomile, neroli, benzoin, bergamot, sandalwood and ylang ylang; place a few drops of any of these oils on a handkerchief and inhale as you prepare yourself for sleep; do not apply these oils to the skin and don't take them internally

Other Ideas

✦ Before bed, spend 10 minutes quietly sitting: no radio, no television, no music, no conversation; reflect on your actions of the day in a calm manner

✦ In bed, spend a few minutes reflecting on the day's activities, but do so in reverse order: getting into bed, getting ready for bed, the events of the evening, those of the afternoon, the morning, rising; some use this technique to fall asleep

✦ Sleep with your head pointing North

✦ Hold, wear, or place beside your bed the following stones: amethyst, aquamarine, blue tourmaline, kunzite, moonstone, lepidolite, peridot. All traditionally produce restful sleep

✦ Stay up later than normal so that you'll be more tired than usual; don't do anything during this period that would stimulate your conscious mind, just relax

✦ Go to bed only when tired and sleepy—not when you feel that you "should" do so

✦ Meditate upon a peaceful concept

✦ Visualize a place of blues, greens, and silvers. Move slowly through this place (it could be a forest at night with the moon shining above)

✦ Listen to soothing music before bed

✦ Read a very dense and uninteresting book before going to bed; don't read in bed, however, on nights of sacred sleep

Appendix 4

DREAM SPELLS

Spells to create specific types of dreams (usually of a prophetic nature) have been popular throughout the world for several millenia. Though some of these rites show Christian influence, their originals pre-date the rise of Christianity.

Dream books often included spells to create dreams. Many persons in Europe had no need of such rites, for they had been handed down as family traditions. Those who lacked access to such information could consult *Mother Bridget's Dream Book* and other such fanciful tomes.[1]

These dream spells betray a remarkable mixture of sources: classical, medieval and folkloric. Celtic and Christian influences also clearly stand out. Some were pure invention. Surprisingly, similar dream spells were found in widely separated countries.[2] The majority of these rites were designed to enable women to ascertain their future husbands.

From Greece: On the eve of St. Catherine's Day (November 26), a young woman makes a loaf of bread, a major ingredient of which is salt. The woman consumes large quantities of the bread as well as a great deal of wine, then falls into bed. In her sleep, the woman will dream of her future mate.[3]

From Scotland: Roast a salted herring, eat it without any other food, speak to no one and drink nothing before going to bed. A person will appear in the dream and offer the dreamer a glass of water. This person is the dreamer's future husband.[4]

From Wales: A sprig of mistletoe is picked on Midsummer Eve. This is placed under the pillow to produce prophetic dreams.[5]

From England (twentieth century): Place a small mirror under your pillow. Sleep on it, and the face of the one you are to marry will appear in a dream.[6]

From England: On Candlemas Eve, three, five, seven, or nine unmarried women gather in a "square chamber." They hang bundles of fresh herbs (including rue and rosemary) in each corner of the room. A cake is made of flour, olive oil, and sugar. Each woman present helps to mix the cake, and contributes to the purchase of its ingredients. The cake is baked. Later, it is cut into equal pieces. Each woman, while cutting her piece, marks it with her initial. The pieces are set before the fire for an hour. Silence is observed during this entire period and the women sit with their arms and knees crossed. Each woman then retrieves her piece of cake and wraps it with a piece of paper on which she has written the love section of the Song of Solomon. This magic bundle is placed beneath her pillow. True dreams regarding her future husband, children, and financial circumstances will follow.[7]

From England: To have true dreams, repeat the following while looking at the moon at night, before bedtime:

> *Luna, every woman's friend,*
> *To me your gladness descend;*
> *Let me, this night, visions see*
> *Emblems of my destiny.*[8]

Notes

Chapter 1: The Mysteries of Dreams

1. MacKenzie, *Dreams and Dreaming*, p. 10.

2. Ibid., p. 47.

3. Domhoff, *The Mystique of Dreams*, p. 2.

4. MacKenzie, op. cit., p. 68.

5. Ibid., p. 43.

6. Evans, *Landscapes of the Night*, p. 76.

7. Domhoff, op. cit, p. 103. For a fascinating survey of the findings of contemporary dream researchers, see Domhoff, Chapter 6.

8. Ibid., p. 97.

Chapter 2: Egypt

1. Shafer, *Religion in Ancient Egypt: Gods, Myths and Personal Practice*, p. 201.

2. Thompson, *The Mystery and Lure of Perfume*, pp. 225–226.

3. Ibid., p. 13.

4. Ibid., p. 13.

5. MacKenzie, *Dreams and Dreaming*, p. 26.

6. Jayne, *The Healing Gods of Ancient Civilizations*, p. 29.

7. Loewe and Blacker, *Oracles and Divination*, p. 75.

8. Jayne, op. cit., p. 30.

9. Shafer, op. cit., p. 171.

10. Romer, *Ancient Lives*, p. 69; MacKenzie, op. cit., pp. 27–28; Evans, *Landscapes of the Night*, p. 47; Loewe and Blacker, op. cit., p. 179.

11. MacKenzie, op. cit., p. 26.

12. Ibid., p. 26.

13. Ibid., p. 29.

14. Hamarkis is the Greek name form for the Egyptian god Harakty, Whose name, in Egyptian, means "Horus Who is on the Horizon." Mercatante, *Who's Who in Egyptian Mythology*, p. 52.

15. Ibid., p. 52.

16. Loewe and Blacker, op. cit., p. 180; MacKenzie, op. cit., p. 52.

17. Brien, *Ancient Egyptian Magic*, p. 215.

18. MacKenzie, op. cit., p. 29.

19. Ibid., pp. 29–30.

20. Shafer, op. cit., p. 185.

21. Jayne, op. cit., p. 30.

22. Ibid., p. 33.

23. MacKenzie, op. cit., p. 30.

24. Brier, op. cit., p. 217.

25. Glass, *They Foresaw the Future*, p. 21.

26. Witt, *Isis in the Graeco-Roman World*, p. 190.

27. Jayne, op. cit., p. 30.

28. Lewisohn, *Science, Prophecy and Prediction*, p. 64.

29. Mercatante, op. cit., pp. 142–143.

30. Witt, op. cit., pp. 185, 189.

31. Glass, op. cit., p. 21.

32. MacKenzie, op. cit., p. 30.

33. Ibid., p. 30.

34. Jayne, op. cit., p. 29.

35. Witt, op. cit., p. 191.

36. Ibid., p. 191.

37. MacKenzie, op. cit., p. 30.

38. Ibid., p. 30.

39. Jayne, op. cit., p. 30.

40. Ibid., p. 30.

41. Ibid., p. 30.

42. Evans, op. cit., p. 47.

43. Jayne, op. cit., p. 30.

44. MacKenzie, op. cit., p. 28.

45. Artemidorus. *The Interpretation of Dreams (Oneirocritica)*, p. 75.

46. Shafer, op. cit., p. 171.

47. Brier, op. cit., p. 217.

48. MacKenzie, op. cit., p. 28; Brier, op. cit., p. 218.

49. Shafer, op. cit., p. 69; Artemidorus, op. cit., p. 75.

50. Brier, op. cit., p. 220.

51. Ibid., p. 218.

52. Shafer, op. cit., p. 170.

53. Brier, op. cit., p. 219.

54. Ibid., p. 219.

55. Ibid., p. 219.

56. Ibid., p. 55.

57. Ibid., p. 219.

58. MacKenzie, op. cit., p. 28.

59. Shafer, op. cit., p. 69.

60. Brier, op. cit., p. 219.

61. Ibid., p. 219.

62. Ibid., p. 219.

63. Ibid., p. 220.

64. Ibid., p. 220.

65. Ibid., p. 219.

66. MacKenzie, op. cit., p. 28.

67. Ibid., p. 28.

68. Ibid., p. 48.

69. Ibid., p. 48.

70. Ibid., p. 48.

71. Ibid., p. 48.

72. Brier, op. cit., p. 223.

73. MacKenzie, op. cit., p. 29.

74. Mercatante, op. cit., p. 39.

75. Ibid., p. 39.

76. Brier, op. cit., pp. 221–222.

77. Mercatante, op. cit., pp. 22–23.

78. Shafer, op. cit., p. 54.

79. Mercatante, op. cit., pp. 22–23.

80. MacKenzie, op. cit., p. 31.

81. Mercatante, op. cit., p. 23.

82. Coxhead and Hiller, *Dreams: Visions of the Night*, p. 27.

83. Brier, op. cit., pp. 221–222.

84. Ibid., pp. 221–222.

85. Ibid., p. 222.

86. Ibid., p. 221.

Chapter 3: The Middle East: Sumeria, Babylon, and Assyria

1. C. F. Kramer, *History Begins at Sumer.*

2. Kramer, *The Sumerians*, p. 5.

3. Ibid., p. 19.

4. Ibid., pp. 21–22.

5. Ibid., 33.

6. Ibid., p. 33–34.

7. Ibid., p. 13.

8. Ibid., p. 113.

9. Ibid., p. 115.

10. Ibid., p. 123.

11. Ibid., p. 123.

12. Ibid., p. 129.

13. Ibid., p. 117.

14. Ibid., p. 117.

15. Ibid., p. 126.

16. Ibid., p. 126.

17. Ibid., p. 135.

18. Ibid., p. 136.

19. Loewe and Blacker, *Oracles and Divination*, p. 143; Delaporte, *Mesopotamia*, p. 155. Much of Delaporte's information actually pertains to Sumer.

20. Loewe and Blacker, op. cit., p. 143.

21. Kramer, op. cit., p. 138.

22. Ibid., p. 38.

23. Delaporte, op. cit., p. 155.

24. Ibid., p. 138–139.

25. Loewe and Blacker, op. cit, p. 157.

26. Ibid., p. 156–157.

27. Finnegan, *Archaeological History of the Ancient Middle East*, p. 40.

28. Ibid., p. 40.

29. Ibid., p. 58.

30. MacKenzie, op. cit., p. 32.

31. Ibid., p. 32.

32. Loewe and Blacker, op. cit., pp. 147–156.

33. MacKenzie, op. cit., p. 32.

34. Hooke, *Babylonian and Assyrian Religion*, p. 83; Jayne, op. cit., p. 101.

35. Loewe and Blacker, op. cit., p. 157.

36. Jayne, op. cit., p. 100.

37. Ibid., p. 101.

38. Delaporte, op. cit., p. 212.

39. Loewe and Blacker, op. cit., 143.

40. Ibid., p. 143.

41. Ibid., p. 143.

42. Oppenheim, "Mantic Dreams in the Ancient Near East," p. 346.

43. Hooke, op. cit., p. 84.

44. Hooke, op. cit., p. 84; Jayne, op. cit., p. 102.

45. Jayne, op. cit., p. 102.

46. Ibid., p. 103.

47. Lurker, *Dictionary of Gods and Goddesses, Devils and Demons*, p. 218; Jayne, op. cit., p. 102.

48. Jayne, op. cit., pp. 100–101.

49. Hooke, op. cit., p. 84.

50. Loewe and Blacker, op. cit., p. 158.

51. Artemidorus, *The Interpretation of Dreams (Oneirocritica)*. p. 73 (note).

52. MacKenzie, op. cit., p. 35.

53. Ibid., p. 48.

54. Ibid., p. 48.

55. Ibid., p. 48.

56. Ibid., p. 48.

57. MacKenzie, op. cit., p. 35.

58. Loewe and Blacker, op. cit., pp. 157–158.

59. Oppenheim, op. cit., pp. 346–347.

60. Ibid., pp. 349–350.

61. MacKenzie, op. cit., p. 34.

62. Dalley, *Myths from Mesopotamia*, p. 328.

63. Sandars, *The Epic of Gilgamesh*, pp. 65–66.

64. Ibid., p. 66.

65. Ibid., p. 66.

66. Ibid., p. 67.

Chapter 4: Greece

1. MacKenzie, op. cit., p. 41.

2. Hippocrates, *Hippocratic Writings*, p. 253.

3. Meier, *The Dream in Ancient Greece and Its Use in Temple Cures* (Incubation), p. 308.

4. Jayne, op. cit., p. 19.

5. Meier, op. cit., 304.

6. Quoted in MacKenzie, op. cit., p. 47.

7. MacKenzie, op. cit., p. 47.

8. Jayne, op. cit., p. 219; Lawson, *Modern Greek Folklore and Ancient Greek Religion*, p. 300.

9. Jayne, op. cit., p. 221.

10. Jayne, op. cit., p. 220; Garfield, *Creative Dreaming*, p. 21.

11. Evans, *Landscapes of the Night*, p. 48.

12. Pausanias, *Guide to Greece*, 492–493; Garfield, op. cit., p. 19; Evans, op. cit., p. 48.

13. Evans, op. cit., p. 48.

14. Jayne, op. cit., p. 279.

15. Meier, op. cit., p. 317.

16. Garfield, op. cit., p. 21.

17. Jayne, op. cit., p. 220.

18. Evans, op. cit., p. 48.

19. Jayne, op. cit., pp. 220; 278–279.

20. Evans, op. cit., p. 48.

21. MacKenzie, op. cit., p. 43.

22. Jayne, op. cit., p. 277.

23. MacKenzie, op. cit., p. 44.

24. Ibid., p. 44.

25. Jayne, op. cit., p. 277.

26. MacKenzie, op. cit., p. 45; Jayne, op. cit., p. 220.

27. Jayne, op. cit., p. 277.

28. Ibid., p. 278.

29. MacKenzie, op. cit., p. 45.

30. Jayne, op. cit., p. 279.

31. MacKenzie, op. cit., p. 43.

32. Ibid., pp. 43; 45.

33. Meier, op. cit., p. 304.

34. Jayne, op. cit., p. 220.

35. MacKenzie, op. cit., p. 43.

36. Ibid., p. 43.

37. MacKenzie, op. cit., p. 44; Lurker, op. cit., pp. 39–40.

38. Smith, *Dictionary of Greek and Roman Biography and Mythology*, Volume 1, p. 46.

39. Jayne, op. cit., p. 282.

40. Meier, op. cit., p. 315.

41. Smith, op. cit., p. 46.

42. Jayne, op. cit., p. 257.

43. Meier, op. cit., p. 316.

44. Jayne, op. cit., p. 292.

45. Jayne, op. cit., p. 293.

46. Hippocrates, op. cit., p. 252.

47. Ibid., p. 256.

48. Ibid., p. 258.

49. Ibid., pp. 257–259.

50. Ibid., p. 256.

51. Artemidorus, op. cit., p. 7.

52. Ibid., pp. 21–22.

53. Smith, I., op. cit., p. 373.

54. Artemidorus, op. cit., p. 21.

55. Ibid., p. 14.

56. Ibid., p. 21.

57. MacKenzie, op. bit., p. 55.

58. Artemidorus, op. cit., p. 27.

59. Ibid., pp. 49–50, 55; 163.

60. bid., pp. 235, 240, 251.

61. Ibid., p. 113.

62. Ibid., p. 114.

63. Ibid., pp. 113–122.

Chapter 5: Rome

1. Jayne, op. cit., p. 393.

2. Ibid., p. 396.

3. MacKenzie, op. cit., p. 50.

4. Ibid., p. 50.

5. Ibid., p. 50.

6. Dill, *Roman Society from Nero to Marcus Aurelius,* p. 457.

7. Ibid., p. 451.

8. MacKenzie, op. cit., p. 52.

9. Dill, op. cit., p. 452.

10. Jayne, op. cit., p. 414.

11. MacKenzie, op. cit., p. 51.

12. Ibid., p. 51.

13. Jayne, op. cit., p. 492.

14. Dill, op. cit., p. 460.

15. Smith, op. cit., Volume 2, p. 137.

16. Jayne, op. cit., p. 421.

17. Ibid., op. cit., p. 422.

18. Smith, op. cit., p. 137.

19. Dill, op. cit., p. 560.

20. Ibid., pp. 461–462.

21. Witt, *Isis in the Graeco-Roman World,* p. 191.

22. Dill, op. cit., p. 563.

23. MacKenzie, op. cit., p. 46.

24. Ibid., p. 47.

Chapter 6: Hawaii

1. Handy and Pukui, *The Polynesian Family System in Ka-'u, Hawai'i*, p. 117.

2. Ibid., pp. 126–127.

3. Pukui, Haertig, Lee, McDermott, *Nana I Ke Kumu*, Volume 2, p. 170.

4. Ibid., p. 170.

5. Ibid., p. 170.

6. Ibid., pp. 170–171; Handy and Pukui, op. cit., pp. 120–122.

7. Pukui, Haertig, Lee, McDermott., op. cit., p. 172.

8. Ibid., p. 176.

9. Ibid., p. 176.

10. Ibid., p. 173.

11. Handy and Pukui, op. cit., p. 9. The traditional Hawaiian "house" consisted of a series of unattached buildings, each of which served a different function: men's eating, women's eating (*hale 'aina*); food storage; canoe shed;

sleeping house.) In many families, the mua also served as a family temple: daily food offerings were made to Lono (god of food and agriculture) and the family's ancestral deities. (Pukui and Handy, op. cit., p. 9.) The Hawaiians also used small outdoor shrines as well.)

12. Ibid., p. 129.

13. Handy, Polynesian Religion, p. 61.

14. Handy and Pukui, op. cit., p. 127.

15. Ibid., p. 99.

16. Pukui, Haertig, Lee, McDermott, op. cit., p. 205.

17. Ibid., p. 205.

18. Kamakau, Ka Po'e Kahiko, p. 56; Pukui, Haertig, Lee, McDermott, op. cit., p. 205.

19. Pukui, Haertig, Lee, McDermott, op. cit., p. 205.

20. Ibid., p. 171.

21. Ibid., p. 77.

22. Ibid., p. 174.

23. Kamakau, op. cit., p. 56.

24. Pukui, Haertig, Lee. McDermott, p. 176.

25. Pukui, 'Olelo No'eau, p. 134.

26. Ibid., p. 186.

27. Ibid., pp. 90; 311.

28. Pukui, Haertig, Lee, McDermott, op. cit., p. 180.

29. Handy and Pukui, op. cit., p. 129.

30. Pukui, op. cit., p. 7.

31. Pukui, Haertig, Lee, McDermott, op. cit., p. 181.

32. Handy and Pukui, p. 128.

Chapter 7: North America

1. Coxhead and Hiller, *Dreams: Visions of the Night*, pp. 66–67.

2. Lincoln, *The Dream in Primitive Cultures*, p. 209.

3. Ibid., p. 209.

4. Ibid., p. 210.

5. Ibid., pp. 210–211.

6. Ibid., 207–208.

7. MacKenzie, op. cit., p. 105.

8. Lincoln, op. cit., pp. 208–209; 212.

9. Ibid., p. 208.

10. Ibid., p. 209.

11. Ibid., p. 209.

12. Ibid., p. 217.

13. Ibid., p. 210.

14. Ibid., p. 217.

15. Ibid., p. 270.

16. Coxhead and Hiller, op. cit., p. 84.

17. Ibid., p. 84.

18. Ibid., p. 84.

19. Garfield, op cit., pp. 75–76.

20. Farb, *Man's Rise to Civilization As Shown by the Indians of North America*, pp. 86–87.

21. Ibid., pp. 86–87.

22. Coxhead and Hiller, op. cit., p. 84.

23. Ibid., p. 12.

24. Corriere, Karle, Woldenberg, Hart, *Dreaming and Waking: The Functional Approach to Dreams*, p. 93.

25. Ibid., p. 94.

26. Ibid., pp. 92–94; Farb, op. cit., p. 132.

27. Wallace, *The Death and Rebirth of the Seneca*, p. 71.

28. Ibid., p. 92.

29. Corriere, Karle, Woldenberg, Hart, op. cit., pp. 99–100; Wallace, op. cit., p. 72.

30. Coxhead and Hiller, op. cit., p. 84.

31. Corrierre, Karle, Woldenberg and Hart., op. cit., p. 94.

32. Ibid., p. 95.

33. MacKenzie, op. cit., p. 106. 34. Coxhead and Hiller, op. cit., p. 12.

35. Ibid., p. 12.

36. Underhill, *The Papago Indians of Arizona and their Relatives, the Pima*, p. 58.

37. Ibid, p. 55.

38. Ibid., pp. 58–59.

39. Ibid., p. 55.

40. Coxhead and Hiller, op. cit., p. 12.

41. Ibid., p. 12.

42. Lincoln, op. cit., p. 266.

43. Highwater, *Ritual of the Wind: North American Indian Ceremonies, Music and Dances*, p. 33.

44. MacKenzie, op. cit., p. 103.

45. Rogers, *The Shaman's Healing Way*, p. 12.

Chapter 8: Dream Books

1. Smith, *Dictionary of Greek and Roman Biography and Mythology*, Volume 1, p. 374.

2. MacKenzie, op. cit., p. 53.

3. Ibid., p. 75.

4. Ibid., p. 77.

5. Ibid., p. 80.

6. Lewisohn, op. cit., pp. 116–117.

7. de Lys, *A Treasury of American Superstitions*, p. 297.

8. MacKenzie, op. cit., pp. 77–79.

Chapter 11: Preparations for Sacred Sleep

1. Taylor, *Red Flower: Rethinking Menstruation*, p. 35.

2. Ibid., pp. 37–38; Shuttle and Redgrove, *The Wise Wound*, p. 92.

3. Shuttle and Redgrove, op. cit., p. 92.

4. Garfield, *Women's Bodies, Women's Dreams*, p. 163.

5. Ibid., p. 163.

6. Ibid., p. 165.

7. Jayne, *The Healing Gods of Ancient Civilizations*, p. 220.

8. Artemidorus, *The Interpretation of Dreams (Onierocritica)*, p. 21.

9. Ibid., p. 70; Jayne, op. cit., p. 278.

10. Jayne, op. cit, p. 278.

11. Ibid, pp. 278–279.

12. Artemidorus, op. cit., p. 70.

13. Hartmann, *The Biology of Dreaming*, p. 51; Garfield, op. cit., p. 27.

14. Taylor, op. cit., p. 38.

15. Hartmann, op. cit., p. 51.

Appendix 4

1. MacKenzie, op. cit., p. 75.

2. Ibid., p. 75.

3. Lawson, *Modern Greek Folklore and Ancient Greek Religion*, p. 303.

4. Opie and Tatern, *A Dictionary of Superstitions*, p. 343.

5. Radford, *Encyclopedia of Superstitions*, p. 105.

6. Haining, *Superstitions*, p. 102.

7. MacKenzie, op. cit., p. 76.

8. Busenbark, *Symbols, Sex and the Stars*, p. 25.

GLOSSARY

CONSCIOUS MIND: That half of human consciousness that operates during waking hours.

CUNEIFORM: Derived from early pictographic writing, cuneiform consists of wedge-shaped marks that, when placed together, form words. Cuneiform was written by pressing the ends of prepared reeds into soft clay tablets and cylinders. It was in wide use in Sumer, Babylon, and Assyria.

DIVINATION: Ritual techniques designed to gain glimpses of distant or future events.

HIERATIC: A form of Egyptian writing, in which the purely pictorial hieroglyphs are written (with ink) in streamlined forms to speed the act of recording information.

INCUBATION, DREAM: An ancient spiritual technique in which worshippers slept in temples to receive dream messages or healing from deities. From the Latin *incubare*. Similar procedures have been practiced throughout history on every continent.

MAGIC: The movement of natural (but little understood) energies from the human body and from natural objects to manifest change. Once a world-wide practice, Christianity attempted to stamp it out because magic placed power in the hands of the people. Early Christians linked magic with "Satan," a false association that continues to this day.

MESSENGER: Our personal deity who comes to us in a dream during sacred sleep bearing important information.

MYTHOLOGY: A demeaning term that refers to the religions of others. I prefer use of the term "sacred stories" to describe the activities of deities. The word "mythology" should not be perceived as referring to false religious concepts, for all religions bear truth.

PAGAN: A person who practices Paganism (q.v.).

PAGANISM: A term in wide use today that describes personal religious activities and constructs in which the pre-Christian deities of many lands are worshipped. Paganism is quite popular, especially among women, as it supports women clergy and is often centered on Goddess worship. Sometimes known as Neo-Paganism.

PERSONAL DEITY: The deity most often worshipped by an individual; or, the only such deity. This concept probably first arose in ancient Sumer.

PSYCHIC MIND: See SUBCONSCIOUS MIND.

REM: Rapid Eye Movement, in which the eyes demonstrate dramatic activity during deep sleep. Once thought to be necessary for dreaming, REM was later recognized as marking merely one of the phases of sleep in which dreaming occurs.

SACRED SLEEP: A word that I've coined to describe the practice of dream incubation at home for specific purposes. The term includes both preparations, ritual and sleep, as well as the interpretation of the received dreams.

SUBCONSCIOUS MIND: That half of our consciousness that operates when we sleep. The subconscious mind is the origin of hunches, intuition, and psychic awareness.

TEMPLE SLEEP: Another term for dream incubation (q.v.).

WICCA: A contemporary Pagan (q.v.) religion in which the divine is worshipped as the Goddess and God. Rituals include the creation of sacred space with magic; invocation to the deities; ritual enactments or celebrations of seasonal phenomena; power-raising (for magic); and a simple meal. Wicca has no links or associations with "Satanism" or other quasi-Christian reactionary groups.

ANNOTATED
BIBLIOGRAPHY

Adler, Margot. *Drawing Down the Moon.* Boston: Beacon Press, 1986. (A compelling survey of contemporary Pagan religious practices.)

Artemidorus. *The Interpretation of Dreams (Oneirocritica).* Translated by Robert J. White. Park Ridge, NJ: Noyes Press, 1975. (This most recent English translation of Artemidorus' classic work clearly demonstrates the breadth and genius of this ancient author. Fascinating reading for anyone with the slightest interest in dreams.

Informed commentaries illuminate the somewhat obscure text.)

Benedict, Ruth. *Patterns of Culture*. New York: Mentor, 1960. (Dreams among Native American peoples.)

Borbely, Alexander. *Secrets of Sleep*. New York: Basic Books, 1986. (Drugs, alcohol, and their effects on sleep and dreaming.)

Brier, Bob. *Ancient Egyptian Magic*. New York: William Morrow, 1980. (Divinely inspired dreams in ancient Egypt; Egyptian dream books; dream interpretation; dream spells and rituals.)

Busenbark, Ernest. *Symbols, Sex and the Stars in Popular Beliefs*. New York: Truth Seeker Press, 1949. (A dream spell is included in Chapter 2.)

Clifford, Terry, and Sam Antupit. *Cures*. New York: Macmillan, 1980. (Remedies for insomnia.)

Contenau, Georges. *Everyday Life in Babylon and Assyria*. New York: Norton, 1966. (Invaluable for divine symbolism and numbers relating to the deities.)

Corriere, Richard. Werner Karle, Lee Woldenberg, and Joseph Hart, *Dreaming and Waking: The Functional Approach To Dreams*. Culver City, CA: Peace Press, 1980. (Chapter 6 contains a remarkably detailed account of Iroquois dream work.)

Coxhead, David and Susan Hiller. *Dreams: Visions of the Night.* New York: Thames and Hudson, 1989. (A short, beautifully illustrated introduction to the spiritual significance of dreams. Much information concerning the importance of dreams to Native American groups.)

Cunningham, Scott. *Magical Aromatherapy: The Power of Scent.* St. Paul: Llewellyn Publications, 1989. (Essential oils that produce sleep when inhaled.)

_____. *Wicca: A Guide for the Solitary Practitioner.* St. Paul: Llewellyn, 1988. (A guide to the religion of Wicca.)

Dalley, Stephanie. *Myths From Mesopotamia.* Oxford, England: Oxford University Press, 1991. (Information concerning Gilgamesh and Mesopotamian deities.)

Davis, Patricia. *Aromatherapy, An A-Z.* Saffron Walden, England: C. W. Daniel, 1988. (Essential oils that induce sleep.)

Delaporte, L. *Mesopotamia: The Babylonian and Assyrian Civilization.* New York: Alfred A. Knopf, 1925. (Early account of Mesopotamia. Book 111,

Chapter 1 contains information concerning the importance of dreams in Babylon and Sumer.)

de Lys, Claudia. *A Treasury of American Superstitions*. New York: Philosophical Library, 1948. (Dream books.)

Dill, Samuel. *Roman Society from Nero to Marcus Aurelius*. New York: Meridian, 1956. (Fine information concerning the worship of Aesculapius and the organization of His temples. In discussing dream interpretation the author displays his bias by describing such practices as "disgusting," "idiotic," "foul" and "profane." Still, his chapter titled "Superstition" is a valuable source of information.)

Domhoff, G. William. *The Mystique of Dreams: A Search for Utopia Through Senoi Dream Therapy*. Berkeley: University of California Press, 1985. (Chapter 6 is a fascinating investigation of the nature of dreams and of dreaming.)

Edwards, I. E. S. editor. *The Cambridge Ancient History: Prolegomena and Prehistory*. Volume 1, Part 1. Cambridge (England): Cambridge University Press, 1980. (Background information concerning the prehistory of Egypt.)

_____. *The Cambridge Ancient History: Early History of the Middle East.* Volume 1, Part 2A. Cambridge (England): Cambridge University Press, 1980. (Background information pertaining to historic Egypt.)

Ehrenwald, Jan, editor. *From Medicine Man to Freud.* New York: Dell, 1956. (Chapter 3 examines healing magic related to sleep and to dreams.)

Evans, Christopher (edited by Peter Evans). *Landscapes of the Night: How and Why We Dream.* New York: Viking Press, 1983. (Chapter 5 contains a fine summary of dreaming in antiquity.)

Farb, Peter. *Man's Rise to Civilization As Shown by the Indians of North America From Primeval Times to the Coming of the Industrial State.* New York: Avon, 1969. (The significance of dreams among the Iroquois and Ojibwa.)

Farrar, Janet and Stewart Farrar. *The Witches' God: Lord of the Dance.* Custer, WA: Phoenix, 1989. (An introduction to aspects of the God as worshipped in both past and present Pagan religions. Part III consists of alphabetical listings of over 1,000 gods.)

_____. *The Witches' Goddess: The Feminine Principle of Divinity.* Custer, WA: Phoenix, 1987.

(A guide to the myriad faces of the Goddess, including a listing of over 1,000 goddesses from around the world.)

Festugiere, Andre-Jean. *Personal Religion Among the Greeks*. Berkeley: University of California Press, 1960. (The importance of dreams in ancient Greek culture; remedies received from Asklepios in dreams. Chapter 5, a discussion of Lucius and Isis, is quite illuminating.)

Finnegan, Jack. *Archaeological History of the Ancient Middle East*. New York: Dorset Press, 1986. (Background information concerning Babylon, Assyria and Egypt.)

Garfield, Patricia. *Creative Dreaming*. New York: Ballantine, 1990. (A lucid look at dreaming in ancient cultures, with suggestions as to how we can utilize certain aspects of these practices in our own dream work.)

_____. *The Healing Power of Dreams*. New York: Simon and Schuster, 1991. (Techniques for using dreams as revealers of unknown health problems and to assist in recovery.)

_____. *Women's Bodies, Women's Dreams*. New York: Ballantine, 1988. (The significance of dreams during every phase of a woman's life, including menstruation and pregnancy.)

Gill, Sam D. *Native American Religions: An Introduction*. Belmont, CA: Wadsworth Publishing, 1982. (Dreams and dreaming among some Native American peoples.)

Glass, Justine. *They Foresaw the Future*. New York: G. P. Putnam's, 1969. (A fascinating history of fulfilled prophecy. Includes chapters on augury in ancient Egypt and Rome.)

Haining, Peter. *Superstitions*. London: Sidgwick and Jackson Limited, 1979. (Dream spells.)

Handy, E. S. Craighill and Mary Kawena Pukui. *The Polynesian Family System in Ka-'u, Hawai'i. 1958*. Reprint. Rutland, VT: Charles E. Tuttle, 1972. (Traditional Hawaiian dream lore.)

Handy, E. S. Craighill. *Polynesian Religion*. Bernice P. Bishop Museum Bulletin 34. 1927. Reprint. Millwood, NY: Kraus, 1985. (Hawaiian dream lore.)

Hartmann, Ernest. *The Biology of Dreaming*. Springfield, IL: Charles C. Thomas, 1967. (This somewhat dated survey contains valuable insights into drugs and their effects on dreaming.)

Highwater, Jamake. *Ritual of the Wind: North American Indian Ceremonies, Music and Dances*.

New York: Viking, 1977. (The importance of dreams to the Pueblo peoples.)

Hippocrates. *Hippocratic Writings.* Edited by G. E. R. Lloyd, translated by J. Chadwick and others. London: Penguin Books, 1983. (The ancient Greek system of diagnosing the nature of ailments according to dream content. An invaluable collection of Hippocratic writings in clear translations.)

Herodotus. *The Histories.* Translated by Aubrey de Selincourt. Baltimore: Penguin Books, 1965. (Background information concerning Graeco-Roman Egypt.)

Hooke, S. H. *Babylonian and Assyrian Religion.* Norman, OK: University of Oklahoma Press, 1962. (Dreams in the ancient world; divine symbolism.)

_____. *Middle Eastern Mythology.* Harmondsworth, England: Penguin Books, 1975. (A valuable introduction to Mesopotamian mythology.)

Jayne, Walter Addison. *The Healing Gods of Ancient Civilizations.* 1925. Reprint. New Hyde Park, NY: University Books, 1962. (Dream incubation in ancient Egypt, Greece, Rome, Babylon and

Assyria. Much information concerning dream deities.)

Kamakau, Samuel Manaiakalani. *Ka Po'e Kahiko*. Honolulu: Bishop Museum Press, 1964. (Dreams and dream interpretation in old Hawai'i.)

Kramer, Samuel Noah. *History Begins at Sumer*. New York: Anchor, 1959. (Background information concerning the Sumerians.)

_____. *Sumerian Mythology: A Study of Spiritual and Literary Achievement in the Third Millenium BC*. New York: Harper Torchbooks, 1961. (Invaluable insights into the nature of Sumerian religion.)

_____. *The Sumerians: Their History, Culture, and Character*. Chicago: University of Chicago Press, 1963. (Chapter 4 is an excellent introduction to Sumerian religion. A few divine dreams are also recorded in this classic work.)

Lawson, John Cuthbert. *Modern Greek Folklore and Ancient Greek Religion*. New Hyde Park, NY: University Books, 1964. (Dreaming among both ancient and contemporary Greeks; a dream spell.)

Lewisohn, Richard. *Science, Prophecy and Prediction*. New York: Premiere, 1962. (Dreams in ancient Egypt; theories of the origins of dreams.)

Lincoln, Jackson Steward. *The Dream In Primitive Cultures*. London: The Cresset Press, 1935. (Part III of this fascinating study discusses dreams and the Navajo, Crow, Blackfoot, Ojibwa, Kwakiutl and other Native American peoples. The information is in-depth and specific. Highly recommended.)

Loewe, Michael, and Carmen Blacker. *Oracles and Divination*. Boulder, CO: Shambhala, 1981. (Dream interpretation in ancient Egypt and Mesopotamia.)

Longworth, T. Clifton. *The Gods of Love: The Creative Process In Early Religion*. Westport, CT: Associated Booksellers, 1960. (Sexual aspects of Pagan religions.)

Lurker, Manfred. *Dictionary of Gods and Goddesses, Devils and Demons*. London: Routledge, 1989. (A comprehensive survey; the best of its kind for finding explicit information concerning deities. Highly recommended.)

MacKenzie, Norman. *Dreams and Dreaming*. New York: The Vanguard Press, 1965. (An invaluable survey of dreaming in ancient cultures around the world. Dream incubation [particularly in Greece and Rome] and the history of dream books are also thoroughly covered.)

McCall, Henrietta. *Mesopotamian Myths*. Austin, TX: the University of Texas Press, 1990. (Gilgamesh information.)

Meier, Carl Alfred. *The Dream in Ancient Greece and Its Use in Temple Cures (Incubation), in The Dream and Human Societies*. Edited by G. E. Von Grunenbaum and Roger Caillois. Berkeley: University of California Press, 1966. (A valuable survey of ancient Greek dream incubation.)

Mercatante, Anthony S. *Who's Who In Egyptian Mythology*. New York: Clarkson N. Potter, 1978. (Egyptian dream deities and dream spells.)

Moscati, Sabatino. *The Face of the Ancient Orient*. New York: Anchor Books, 1960. (Background information concerning Egypt.)

Oates, Joan. *Babylon*. London: Thames and Hudson, 1979. (Background information regarding The Epic of Gilgamesh.)

Opie, Iona and Moira Tatem, editors. *A Dictionary of Superstitions*. Oxford, England: Oxford University Press, 1989. (Dream spells.)

Oppenheim, A. Leo. "Mantic Dreams in the Ancient Near East," in *The Dream and Human Society*. Edited by G. E. Von Grunebaurn and

Roger Caillois. Berkeley: University of California Press, 1966. (An informed survey of dream interpretation in Mesopotamia.)

Pausanias. *Guide to Greece.* Three volumes. Harmondsworth, England: Penguin Books, 1971. (This translation of Pausanias' classic record of ancient Greek temples contains references to Isian dream sanctuaries. Fascinating reading, though it is over 2,000 years old.)

Plutarch. *De Iside Et Osiride (Isis and Osiris).* Translated by J. Gwyn Griffiths. Wales: University of Wales Press, 1970. (Plutarch's long neglected account of Isian and Serapian worship in the Roman world receives an informed translation. Plutarch includes many old world sites connected with Their worship.)

Price, A. Grenfell, editor. *The Explorations of Captain James Cook in the Pacific As Told by Selections of His Own Journals, 1768–1779.* New York: Dover, 197 1. (Ancient Hawaiian culture.)

Pukui, Mary Kawena. *'Olelo No'eau: Hawaiian Proverbs and Poetical Sayings.* Bernice P. Bishop Museum Special Publication No. 71. Honolulu: Bishop Museum Press, 1983. (Interpretations of common Hawaiian cultural dreams.)

Pukui, Mary Kawena, and Samuel H. Elbert. *Hawaiian Dictionary.* Honolulu: University of Hawai'i Press, 1986. (Hawaiian orthography.)

Pukui, Mary Kawena, E. W. Haertig,, and Catherine A. Lee. *Nana I Ke Kumu.* Volume 1. Honolulu: Queen Lili'uokalani Children's Center, 1983. (The significance of dreams in ancient Hawai'i.)

_____. *Nana I Ke Kumu.* Volume 2. Honolulu: Queen Lili'uokalani Children's Center, 1979. (An astounding range of information relating to Hawaiian dreams and to dream interpretation.)

Radford, Edwin and Mona A. *Encyclopedia of Superstitions.* New York: Philosophical Library, 1949. (Dream spells.)

Rogers, Spencer L. *The Shaman's Healing Way.* Ramona, CA: Acoma Books, 1976. (Dreams among the Paviotso people of North America.)

Romer, John. *Ancient Lives: Daily Life in Egypt of the Pharaohs.* New York: Henry Holt and Company, 1990. (An immensely enjoyable, easily read recreation of daily life in a small village of Egyptian artisans circa 1600 B.C.E. Chapter 10 examines the significance of dreams and, from the extant material, the author ingeniously uncovers the hopes and concerns of this distant people.)

Rose, Jeanne. *Herbs and Things: Jeanne Rose's Herbal.* New York: Perigee, 1983. (Herbs for insomnia.)

_____. *The Modern Herbal.* New York: Perigee, 1987. (More remedies for insomnia.)

Sandars, N. K. (translator and commentator). *The Epic of Gilgamesh.* Harmondsworth, England: Penguin Books, 1975. (A fine translation with valuable discussions concerning the history of the poem as well as its major themes. Highly recommended.)

Shafer, Byron E., editor. *Religion in Ancient Egypt: Gods, Myths and Personal Practice.* Ithaca, NY: Cornell University Press, 1991. (An up-to-date look at aspects of both state and private religious practices and beliefs in ancient Egypt.)

Shuttle, Penelope and Peter Redgrove. *The Wise Wound: The Myths, Realities, and Meanings of Menstruation.* (A pioneering study of menstruation. Chapter III discusses its influence on dreams.)

Smith, William. *Dictionary of Greek and Roman Biography and Mythology.* Three volumes. London: Taylor and Walton, 1844. (Invaluable for the attributes, appearances, and symbolism of Greek and Roman deities.)

Bibliography

Taylor, Dena. *Red Flower: Rethinking Menstruation.*
Freedom, CA: The Crossing Press, 1988.
(Chapter 3 examines the role of dreams just
before and during menarche and menstruation.)

Thompson, C. J. S. *The Magic of Perfumes.* New
York: J. B. Lippincott, 1927. (Chapters 2, 6, and
22 contain valuable information concerning the
use of perfume and incense in ancient Egypt.)

Tierra, Lesley. *The Herbs of Life: Health and Healing
Using Western and Chinese Techniques.* Freedom,
CA: The Crossing Press, 1992. (Herbs for
insomnia.)

Underhill, Ruth. *The Papago Indians of Arizona and
their Relatives The Pima.* Washington, DC: The
Bureau of Indian Affairs, ND. (Papago
concerns that dreams cause illness.)

Von Grunebaum, G. E., and Roger Caillois,
editors. *The Dream and Human Societies.*
Berkeley: University of California Press, 1966.
(A survey of dreaming in many ancient and
modern cultures.)

Wallace, Anthony F. C. *The Death and Rebirth of
the Seneca.* New York: Vintage Books, 1972.
(Chapter 3 contains an account of Iroquois
dream work.)

Witt, R. E. *Isis in the Graeco-Roman World.* Ithaca, NY: Cornell University Press, 1971. (Dream incubation in the temples of Isis; dreaming in ancient Egypt and Rome.)

INDEX

☾ REACH FOR THE MOON

Llewellyn publishes hundreds of books on your favorite subjects! To get these exciting books, including the ones on the following pages, check your local bookstore or order them directly from Llewellyn.

ORDER BY PHONE
- Call toll-free within the U.S. and Canada, 1–800–THE MOON
- In Minnesota, call (651) 291–1970
- We accept VISA, MasterCard, and American Express

ORDER BY MAIL
- Send the full price of your order (MN residents add 7% sales tax) in U.S. funds, plus postage & handling to:

  Llewellyn Worldwide
  P.O. Box 64383, Dept. K192–9
  St. Paul, MN 55164–0383, U.S.A.

POSTAGE & HANDLING
(For the U.S., Canada, and Mexico)
- $4.00 for orders $15.00 and under
- $5.00 for orders over $15.00
- No charge for orders over $100.00

We ship UPS in the continental United States. We ship standard mail to P.O. boxes. Orders shipped to Alaska, Hawaii, The Virgin Islands, and Puerto Rico are sent first-class mail. Orders shipped to Canada and Mexico are sent surface mail.

International orders: Airmail—add freight equal to price of each book to the total price of order, plus $5.00 for each non-book item (audio tapes, etc.).

Surface mail—Add $1.00 per item.

Allow 2 weeks for delivery on all orders.
Postage and handling rates subject to change.

DISCOUNTS
We offer a 20% discount to group leaders or agents. You must order a minimum of 5 copies of the same book to get our special quantity price.

FREE CATALOG: Get a free copy of our color catalog, *New Worlds of Mind and Spirit.* Subscribe for just $10.00 in the United States and Canada ($30.00 overseas, airmail). Many bookstores carry *New Worlds*—ask for it!

Visit our web site at www.llewellyn.com for more information.

Cunningham's
ENCYCLOPEDIA OF CRYSTAL, GEM & METAL MAGIC
Scott Cunningham

Here you will find the most complete information anywhere on the magical qualities of more than 100 crystals and gemstones, as well as several metals. The information for each crystal, gem, or metal includes: its related energy, planetary rulership, magical element, deities, Tarot Card, and the magical powers that each is believed to possess. Also included is a complete description of their uses for magical purposes. The classic on the subject.

**240 pp., 6 x 9
illus., color plates
softcover**

**0–87542–126–1
$14.95**

Cunningham's
ENCYCLOPEDIA OF MAGICAL HERBS
Scott Cunningham

The most comprehensive source of herbal data for magical uses ever printed! Almost every one of the over 400 herbs are illustrated, a great source for herb identification, as well as: magical properties, planetary rulerships, genders, associated deities, folk and Latin names, and much more. It also contains a folk name cross reference, and all of the herbs are fully indexed.

Like all of Cunningham's books, this one does not require complicated rituals or expensive magical paraphernalia. Instead, it shares with you the intrinsic powers of the herbs, assisting you to discover which herbs can be used for luck, love, success, money, divination, astral projection, safety, psychic self-defense and much more. This book is a classic in its field—a must for all Wiccans.

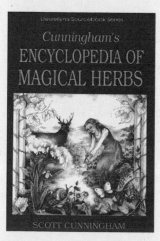

**336 pp., 6 x 9
illus., softcover
0–87542–122–9
$14.95**

EARTH, AIR, FIRE & WATER
More Techniques of Natural Magic

Scott Cunningham

A water-smoothed stone . . . The wind . . . A candle's flame . . . A pool of water. These are the age-old tools of natural magic. Born of the Earth, possessing inner power, they await only our touch and intention to bring them to life.

The four Elements are the ancient powerhouses of magic. Using their energies, we can transform ourselves, our lives, and our worlds. Tap into the marvelous powers of the natural world with more than 75 rites, spells, and simple rituals that you can do easily and with a minimum of equipment. *Earth, Air, Fire & Water* includes detailed instructions for designing your own magical spells. This book instills a sense of wonder concerning our planet and our lives; and promotes a natural, positive practice that anyone can successfully perform.

240 pp., 5¼ x 8
illus., softcover
0–897542–131–8
$9.95

EARTH POWER
Techniques of Natural Magic

Scott Cunningham

Magick is the art of working with the forces of Nature to bring about necessary and desired changes. The forces of Nature—expressed through Earth, Air, Fire and Water—are our "spiritual ancestors" who paved the way for our emergence from the prehistoric seas of creation. Attuning to and working with these energies in magick not only lends you the power to affect changes in your life, it also allows you to sense your own place in the larger scheme of Nature.

Using the "Old Ways" enables you to live a better life and to deepen your understanding of the world. The tools and powers of magick are around you, waiting to be grasped and utilized. This book gives you the means to put Magick into your life, shows you how to make and use the tools, and gives you spells for every purpose.

**176 pp., 5¼ x 8
illus., softcover**

0–87542–121–0
$9.95

To order, call 1–800–THE MOON
Prices subject to change without notice.

MAGICAL HERBALISM
The Secret Craft of the Wise

Scott Cunningham

Certain plants are prized for the special range of energies—the vibrations, or powers—they possess. *Magical Herbalism* unites the powers of plants and man to produce change in accord with human will and desire.

This is the Magic of amulets and charms, sachets and herbal pillows, incenses and scented oils, simples and infusions and anointments, an art that anyone can learn and enjoy as we rediscover our roots and make inner connections with the world of Nature.

This is a special kind of Magic that is beautiful and natural—that does not use the medicinal powers of herbs, but rather the subtle vibrations and scents that work at the causal level behind the material world.

This book includes step-by-step guidance to the use of herbs, with simple spells for every purpose.

260 pp., 5¼ x 8
illus., softcover

0–87542–120–2
$9.95

HERB MAGIC VIDEO
with Scott Cunningham

This is the ultimate home-study course in herbalism from master herbalist Scott Cunningham. You'll learn to harvest and cure natural herbs; prepare ancient recipes for magical incense, sachets and talismans; and create pure herbal essences and tinctures. You and Scott will visit a working herb farm to learn how to identify many common and rare herbs on sight. Discover and use the power of herb magic and spells—secrets that are revealed here for the very first time. It is often easier to learn something by having it demonstrated to you than it is when you read about it in a book. With this videotape, Cunningham gives you a personal lesson in herb magic!

HERB
Magic
featuring
SCOTT CUNNINGHAM

*Learn expert secrets for creating your own
enchanting magical oils, incenses, sachets,
powders, tinctures, and bath salts.*

**American VHS only
60 min.**

**0–87542–117–2
$29.95**

LIVING WICCA
A Further Guide for the Solitary Practitioner
Scott Cunningham

Living Wicca is the long-awaited sequel to Scott Cunningham's wildly successful *Wicca: a Guide for the Solitary Practitioner.* This book is for those who have made the conscious decision to bring Wiccan spirituality into their everyday lives. It provides solitary practitioners with the tools and added insights that will enable them to blaze their own spiritual paths—to become their own high priests and priestesses.

Unlike any other book on the subject, *Living Wicca* is a step-by-step guide to creating your own Wiccan tradition and personal vision of the gods, designing your personal ritual and symbols, developing your own book of shadows, and truly living your Craft.

208 pp., 6 x 9
llus., softcover
0–87542–184–9
$12.95

To order, call 1–800–THE MOON
Prices subject to change without notice.

MAGICAL AROMATHERAPY
The Power of Scent

Scott Cunningham

Scent magic has a rich, colorful history. Today, in the shadow of the next century, there is much we can learn from the simple plants that grace our planet. Most have been used for countless centuries. The energies still vibrate within their aromas.

Scott Cunningham has combined knowledge of the physiological and psychological effects of natural fragrances with the ancient art of magical perfumery. *Magical Aromatherapy* contains a wealth of practical tables of aromas of the seasons, days of the week, the planets, and zodiac; use of essential oils with crystals; synthetic and genuine oils and hazardous essential oils. It also contains a handy appendix of aromatherapy organizations and distributors of essential oils and dried plant products.

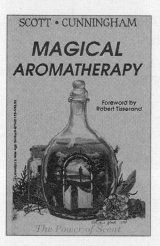

SCOTT • CUNNINGHAM

MAGICAL AROMATHERAPY

Foreword by
Robert Tisserand

The Power of Scent

224 pp., mass market, illus.

0–87542–129–6
$3.95

THE MAGICAL HOUSEHOLD
Empower Your Home with Love, Protection, Health and Happiness

Scott Cunningham and David Harrington

Whether your home is a small apartment or a palatial mansion, you want it to be something special. Now it can be with *The Magical Household*. Learn how to make your home more than just a place to live. Turn it into a place of security, life, fun, and magic. Here you learn simple, quick and effective magical spells that use nothing more than common items in your house: furniture, windows, doors, carpet, pets, etc. You will learn to make magic a part of your life. The result is a home that is safeguarded from harm and a place which will bring you happiness, health and much more.

**208 pp., 5¼ x 8
illus., softcover**

**0–87542–124–5
$9.95**

DREAMS AND WHAT THEY MEAN TO YOU

Migene González Wippler

Everyone dreams, yet dreams are rarely taken seriously. In this fascinating book, the author gives you all of the information needed to begin interpreting—even creating—your own dreams.

Dreams and What They Mean To You discusses the results of the most recent scientific research on sleep and dreams. The author analyzes different types of dreams: telepathic, nightmares, sexual and prophetic. In addition, there is an extensive Dream Dictionary listing the meanings of hundreds of dream images.

Then, González-Wippler tells you how to practice creative dreaming—consciously controlling dreams as you sleep will expand horizons and increase success!

240 pp., mass market
0–87542–288–8
$4.99

SPELL CRAFTS
Creating Magical Objects

Scott Cunningham & David Harrington

Since early times, crafts have been intimately linked with spirituality. When crafts were used to create objects intended for ritual or that symbolized the Divine, the connection between the craftsperson and divinity grew more intense. Today, handcrafts can still be more than a pastime—they can be rites of power and honor; a religious ritual. After all, hands were our first magical tools.

Spell Crafts is a modern guide to creating physical objects for the attainment of specific magical goals. It is far different from magic books that explain how to use purchased magical tools. Learn how to fashion spell brooms, weave wheat, dip candles, sculpt clay, mix herbs, bead sacred symbols, and much more

224 pp., 5¼ x 8
illus., photos
0–87542–185–7
$10.00

To order, call 1–800–THE MOON
Prices subject to change without notice.

WHAT YOUR DREAMS CAN TEACH YOU

Alex Lukeman

The new, expanded edition of *What Your Dreams Can Teach You* is a workbook of self-discovery, with a systematic and proven approach to the understanding of dreams. It does not contain lists of meanings for dream symbols. Only you, the dreamer, can discover what the images in your dreams mean for you. The book does contain step-by-step information which can lead you to success with your dreams, success that will bear fruit in your waking hours. Learn to tap into the aspect of yourself that truly knows how to interpret dreams, the inner energy of understanding called the "Dreamer Within." This aspect of your consciousness will lead you to an accurate understanding of your dreams and even assist you with interpreting the dreams of others.

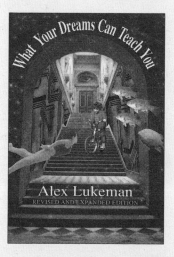

336 pp., 6 x 9
softcover
0–87542–475–9
$14.95

WHISPERS OF THE MOON
The Life & Work of Scott Cunningham

David Harrington & deTraci Regula

Scott Cunningham (b. 1956–d. 1993) wrote more than 50 books, 15 of which lay the foundation for the non-institutional growth of modern Wicca. Tens of thousands of new Wiccans cast their first magic circle using his words of power. Scott also opened up a new understanding of positive, nature-based magics such as herb, gem and elemental magic.

Scott's unfinished autobiography, *Whispers of the Moon*, was completed by two of his closest friends. While the book traces his life and growth as a writer as well as a philosopher-magician, it also includes some of Scott's poetry, portions of letters, and exposition of his personal philosophy and religion.

272 pp., 6 x 9
photos, softcover
1–56718–559–2
$15.00

To order, call 1–800–THE MOON
Prices subject to change without notice.

WICCA
A Guide for the Solitary Practitioner

Scott Cunningham

Wicca is a book of life, and how to live magically, spiritually, and wholly attuned with Nature. It is a book of sense and common sense, not only about Magick, but about religion and one of the most critical issues of today: how to achieve a wholesome relationship with our Earth. Cunningham presents Wicca as it is today: a gentle, Earth-oriented religion dedicated to the Goddess and God.

Here is a positive, practical introduction to the religion of Wicca, designed so that any interested person can learn to practice the religion alone, anywhere in the world, presenting Wicca honestly and clearly. It shows that Wicca is a vital, satisfying part of twentieth century life.

**240 pp., 6 x 9
illus., softcover**

**0–87542–118–0
$9.95**

Did You Know?

Many of Scott Cunningham's books are also available in Spanish! Now you can recommend your favorite Cunningham titles to your Spanish-reading friends.

Choose from these:

Enciclopedia de cristales, gemas y metales mágicos (1–56718–189–9, $14.95 U.S.)

Enciclopedia de las hierbas mágicas (1–56718–883–4, $12.95 U.S.)

Inciensos, aceites e infusiones (1–56718–930–X, $9.95 U.S.)

La casa mágica: fortalezca su hogar con amor, salud y felicidad (1–56718–931–8, $7.95 U.S.)

La verdad sobre la brujeria (1–56718–878–8, $1.99 U.S.)

La verdad sobre la mágia de las hierbas (1–56718–875–3, $1.99 U.S.)

Llewellyn Español

To order, call 1–800–THE MOON
Prices subject to change without notice.